Multiple Choice Questions in Advanced Level Chemistry

Multiple Choice Questions in Advanced Level Chemistry

JOHN BIGGS
Department of Chemistry
University of Hull

PETER SIMPSON
School of Chemistry and Molecular Sciences
University of Sussex

Test Development and Research Unit
Objective Test Series

General Editor
John S. Hamilton

CAMBRIDGE
UNIVERSITY PRESS

Published by the Press Syndicate of the University of Cambridge
The Pitt Building, Trumpington Street, Cambridge CB2 1RP
40 West 20th Street, New York, NY 10011–4211, USA
10 Stamford Road, Oakleigh, Melbourne 3166, Australia

on behalf of the Oxford and Cambridge Schools Examination Board, the University of
Cambridge Local Examinations Syndicate and the Test Development and Research Unit of the
Cambridge, Oxford and Southern School Examinations Council.

First published 1985
Reprinted 1993

Printed in Great Britain by the
Athenaeum Press Ltd, Newcastle upon Tyne

Library of Congress catalogue card number: 82-14607

British library cataloguing in publication data

Biggs, John
Multiple choice questions in advanced level
chemistry. – (Test Development and Research
Unit objective test series)
1. Chemistry – Examinations, questions, etc.
I. Title   II. Simpson, Peter   III. Series
540′.76   QD42

ISBN 0 521 31693 6

Contents

vi   CONTENTS

General Introduction

This series arises from the work of the Test Development and Research Unit in the development and production of objective tests, and it is based on the belief that good objective tests have an educational as well as a measurement function. The Unit has always considered that a good test item (question) should not only possess the qualities of conciseness, clarity and originality, but that it should also be of a kind which teachers would like to have for teaching purposes and which students would find of real interest.

The test items included in this series originated as part of a larger number of items which were rigorously scrutinised, edited and pretested to ensure their relevance to the study of the subjects at the stated levels, and to permit the measures of their facility and discrimination (discussed elsewhere in this book) to be estimated in advance. Thus only the best of the original items are included in actual G.C.E. examinations, and it is from this stock of examination items that the present series has been compiled.

The items have two main uses for students. First, an objective test can provide a learning experience. Although most items in examinations are intended to discriminate effectively between candidates of different abilities, it is the examiners' policy to include some items which, although likely to yield comparatively low facility and discrimination indices, seem particularly useful in presenting novel situations and unusual problems. Such items expand the students' knowledge, whilst more familiar items consolidate the knowledge they already possess.

Second, and with the help of the statistics presented, it is possible to compare the performance of pre-examination students with that of examination candidates. If the abilities of individual students are to be evaluated reliably, however, a test containing at least thirty items should be used.

In preparing this series I have had much useful advice and criticism from experienced examiners and teachers, and from colleagues among the staffs of the Test Development and Research Unit and the examination boards. The editors of the individual books have taken great care in the task of presenting the best possible materials to students and teachers. Despite the complexities of editing and pretesting, our experience is that the most essential ingredient of good objective tests is the provision of good items as raw material, and the writing of objective test items is a skilled and often underrated task. Grateful acknowledgement is therefore made to all those who have contributed items to the boards' examinations, and I hope that this series will allow their efforts to be more widely appreciated.

John S. Hamilton
Test Development and Research Unit

Introduction

The multiple choice items in this book are taken from recent A-level Chemistry examinations set by the University of Cambridge Local Examinations Syndicate and the Oxford and Cambridge Schools Examination Board. We would hope that this compilation will be of use to students who will be taking A-level examinations and to all students who will be taking similar examinations or who wish to embark upon studies involving chemistry at universities and polytechnics. Obviously, however, some of the items presented will not be applicable to certain syllabuses at this level.

The booklet is arranged in seven sections. Each of the sections A to D contains four exercises and each of the sections E to G three exercises. The last two exercises in each section are the more difficult.

All exercises contain ten items. The majority contain only simple completion items, but eleven of the exercises (A2, A4, B2, B4, C2, C4, D2, D4, E3, F3, G3) incorporate a number of multiple completion items (see the back page for an explanation of these two types of item).

The subject has been divided into four broad areas.

A   General and physical chemistry I
  Relative masses of atoms and molecules; empirical and molecular formulae
  Atomic structure; radioactivity; periodicity related to atomic structure
  The nature of chemical bonding
  The shapes of simple molecules; stereochemistry in organic molecules; chirality
  Lattice structure of solids
  The gaseous state

B   General and physical chemistry II
  Chemical equilibria, including ionic, phase and redox equilibria; pH and acidity; solutions; osmosis
  Reaction kinetics and catalysis
  Chemical thermodynamics: enthalpy changes and Hess's Law; Born–Haber cycles

C   Inorganic chemistry
  The Periodic Table; periodicity of chemical and physical properties
  Hydrogen; Groups I, II, IV, VII; aluminium; nitrogen and phosphorus; oxygen and sulphur; *d*-block elements

2

D *Organic chemistry*
   Reaction mechanisms
   The properties of simple organic compounds: hydrocarbons, and
     halogen, hydroxy, carbonyl and nitrogen compounds
   Polymers

   Exercises A, B, C and D correspond directly to the four topic areas
   Exercises E combine topic areas A and B
   Exercises F combine topic areas C and D
   Exercises G combine all four topic areas

The items have been chosen to test a wide range of skills. Some of the items test the ability to recognise and recall a piece of information: the properties of a compound or the statement of a theory. Others require the use of information that is presented in a familiar way; a calculation or a routine deduction is demanded. More complex items present unfamiliar situations in which students are required to search in their minds for the appropriate law or property necessary for the solution of the problem, and to perceive relationships which are new to them. To some extent, the precise skill classification of an item will depend upon the syllabus a student has followed. A balance within each exercise has been sought, however, by reference to the skill classifications used by the two boards whose items have been drawn upon.

Each of the exercises should be completed by well-prepared candidates within 20 minutes: typical examination times are $1\frac{1}{4}$ hours for a 40-item test, and $1\frac{3}{4}$ hours for a 50-item test. The items are reproduced largely in the form in which they appeared in A-level examinations.

In recent years there have been changes in terminology and nomenclature. We draw attention to the Joint Statement to Schools by the G.C.E. boards, made in June 1973, and reproduced in *Chemical Nomenclature, Symbols and Terminology*, published by The Association for Science Education, 1979, pp. 81–2. For the sake of clarity, we have commonly inserted the traditional name after the recommended name.

                                             John Biggs and Peter Simpson

SECTION A GENERAL AND PHYSICAL CHEMISTRY I

EXERCISE 1

A 1.1 What is the particle X in the following nuclear reaction?

$$^{27}_{13}\text{Al} + ^{1}_{0}\text{n} \rightarrow X + ^{4}_{2}\text{He}$$

A $^{24}_{10}\text{Ne}$ **B** $^{24}_{11}\text{Na}$ **C** $^{24}_{12}\text{Mg}$ **D** $^{23}_{11}\text{Na}$ **E** $^{24}_{14}\text{Si}$

A 1.2 Which one of the following compounds exhibits cis-/trans-
(geometric) isomerism?
A $CH_2{=}CHCO_2H$
B $HO_2CCH{=}CHCO_2H$
C $CH_2{=}C(CH_3)CO_2H$
D $CH_2{=}CHCH_3$
E $CH_2{=}CH(CH_2)_3CH_3$

A 1.3 The element with electronic configuration [Ar] $3d^{10}\,4s^2\,4p^2$ belongs
to a group of the Periodic Table the first member of which is
A beryllium. **B** boron. **C** carbon.
D nitrogen. **E** oxygen.

A 1.4 The length of a carbon–carbon bond in a saturated aliphatic
compound is 0.154 nm, whereas that of the carbon–carbon double
bond is 0.134 nm. Within the benzene molecule, the interatomic
distance between adjacent carbon atoms is likely to be
A 0.124 nm **B** 0.134 nm **C** 0.139 nm **D** 0.160 nm
E 0.154 nm for three bonds and 0.134 nm for the remaining three

A 1.5 Which one of the following species has a planar molecular
structure?
A NH_3 **B** BF_3 **C** NH_4^+ **D** H_3O^+ **E** CH_4

A 1.6 Study the table of electronic structures of the five elements listed
below. Which element is likely to be the most inert?

	electronic structure
Element **A**	2, 8, 1
Element **B**	2, 8, 8
Element **C**	2, 8, 16, 2
Element **D**	2, 8, 18, 7
Element **E**	2, 8, 18, 18, 8

4

A 1.7   A diver should always breathe oxygen at a partial pressure of 20 kPa. What percentage of oxygen by volume should his breathing mixture contain when he dives to a depth of 40 m and the pressure on him rises to 500 kPa?

A   20%   B   10%   C   8%   D   5%   E   4%

A 1.8   The number of isomers of molecular formula $C_2H_4Br_2$ is

A   1   B   2   C   3   D   4   E   5

A 1.9   For which one of the following solutes has a 0.01 mol dm^{-3} solution the greatest number of ions per unit volume?

A $KAl(SO_4)_2 . 12H_2O$
B $CuCl_2 . 2H_2O$
C $FeSO_4 . (NH_4)_2SO_4 . 24H_2O$
D $La(NO_3)_3$
E $NH_4NaHPO_4 . 4H_2O$

A 1.10   Complete combustion of a sample of a hydrocarbon Q gave 0.66 g of carbon dioxide and 0.36 g of water. [Relative atomic masses: H, 1.0; C, 12; O, 16.] The empirical formula of Q is

A CH_2 B C_3H_4 C C_3H_5 D C_3H_8 E C_6H_8

EXERCISE 2

A 2.1   What is the formula of the isotope produced by the emission of a β-particle from the isotope of phosphorus $^{32}_{15}P$?

A $^{28}_{13}Al$ B $^{31}_{15}P$ C $^{31}_{16}S$ D $^{32}_{16}S$ E $^{32}_{14}Si$

A 2.2   How many electrons e are required to balance the following equation?

$$XO_3^- + 6H^+ + \ldots e \rightarrow X^- + 3H_2O$$

A   0   B   2   C   3   D   4   E   6

6 EXERCISE 2

A 2.3   Which one of the elements **A, B, C, D** or **E**, shown in the graph below is an alkali metal? (The atomic number increases in unit steps.)

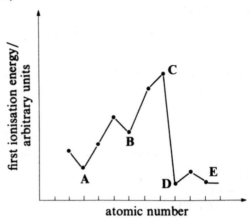

A 2.4   Which one of the following compounds does *not* contain an asymmetric carbon atom?

A

$$CH_3 \diagdown \quad \diagup H$$
$$C$$
$$HO \diagup \quad \diagdown CN$$

B

$$CO_2H$$
$$H—C—OH$$
$$H—C—OH$$
$$CO_2H$$

C

$$CO_2H$$
$$H—C—OH$$
$$H—C—OH$$
$$CH_3$$

D

OH ... OH
$$C$$
$$HO \quad CH_3$$

E

OH ... OH
$$C$$
$$HO \quad CO_2C_2H_5$$

A 2.5   How many chloride ions are in contact with each sodium ion in the crystal of sodium chloride?

    A 1   **B** 2   **C** 4   **D** 6   **E** 8

A 2.6   The following equation represents the catalytic decomposition of H_2O_2:

$$2H_2O_2 \text{ (l)} \xrightarrow{\text{Pt}} 2H_2O \text{ (l)} + O_2 \text{ (g)}$$

What volume of O_2 (g), measured at s.t.p., can be obtained from the catalytic decomposition of 1.0 dm³ of 0.50 mol dm⁻³ H_2O_2?

A   0.5 dm³   B   5.6 dm³   C   11.2 dm³
D   5.6/34 dm³   E   11.2/34 dm³

A 2.7   The bond lengths and bond angles in the molecules of methane, ammonia, and water may be represented as follows:

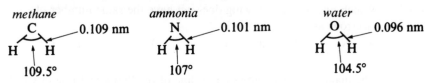

This variation in bond angle is due to

1   the increasing repulsion between hydrogen atoms as the bond length decreases.
2   the number of non-bonding electron pairs in the molecule.
3   a non-bonding electron pair having a greater repulsive force than a bonding electron pair.

A 2.8   Which of the following tests, when used alone, are capable of distinguishing between the compounds $CH_3N{=}NCH_3$ (relative molecular mass 58), $CH_3CH_2CH{=}CH_2$ (r.m.m. 56) and $CH_3CH_2CH_2OH$ (r.m.m. 60)?

1   measurement, at a known pressure and temperature, of the density of a gaseous sample
2   measurement of the mass of carbon dioxide produced when a known mass of the compound is burnt in an excess of oxygen
3   measurement, at a known pressure and temperature, of the rate of effusion of a gaseous sample

A 2.9   In an experiment, 10 cm³ of a gaseous organic compound Y required 25 cm³ of oxygen for complete combustion, both volumes being measured at the same temperature and pressure. Which of the following are possible formulae for Y?

1   CH_4 2 C_2H_2 3 CH_3CHO

A 2.10   In which of the following organic structures do all the carbon atoms lie in one plane?

1   [benzene ring with ${-}CH_3$]   2 $CH_3{-}C{\equiv}C{-}CH_3$ 3 $CH_3{-}\underset{\underset{CH_3}{|}}{\overset{\overset{CH_3}{|}}{C}}{-}CH_3$

EXERCISE 3

A 3.1   The ground state electronic configuration of the element which is isoelectronic with H_2S is

A $1s^2\, 2s^2\, 2p^6$
B $1s^2\, 2s^2\, 2p^6\, 3s^2$
C $1s^2\, 2s^2\, 2p^6\, 3s^2\, 3p^2$
D $1s^2\, 2s^2\, 2p^6\, 3s^2\, 3p^4$
E $1s^2\, 2s^2\, 2p^6\, 3s^2\, 3p^6$

A 3.2   Which one of the following does *not* have the same number of electrons as a fluoride ion F^-?

A   Ne   B H_2O C Na^+ D Al^{3+} E Li^+

A 3.3   The diagram below shows an outline of the Periodic Table in which certain elements are indicated by letters which are *not* their usual symbols.

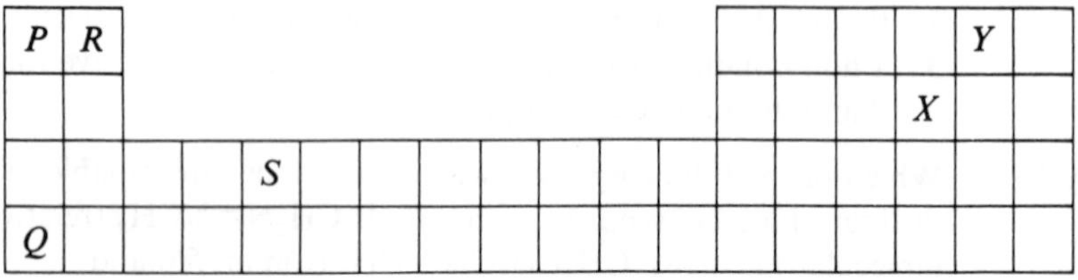

In each of the pairs below, the elements combine together. For which one of the pairs does the bond in the compound produced possess the greatest ionic character?

A P and X B P and Y C Q and Y
D R and X E S and Y

A 3.4   In which one of the following pairs is the radius of the second atom greater than that of the first atom?

A   Na, Mg   B   Sr, Ca   C   Br, Cl   D   Si, P
E   N, P

A 3.5   Which one of the following compounds would be expected to be the most strongly ionic in character?

A $BaCl_2$ B BaI_2 C $CaBr_2$ D $CaCl_2$
E $SrCl_2$

A 3.6   In the emission line spectrum of hydrogen, how many lines can be accounted for by all the possible electron transitions between the five levels of lowest energy within the atom?

    A 4   **B** 5   **C** 8   **D** 10   **E** 20

A 3.7   The relative strengths of the hydrogen-bonds between the molecules in liquid hydrogen halides H—X can best be illustrated by comparison of

    A   the enthalpy changes of vaporisation.
    B   the enthalpy changes of formation.
    C   the freezing points.
    D   the H—X bond energies.
    E   the enthalpy changes of solvation.

A 3.8 X, Y and Z are elements in the same short period. The oxide of X is a giant molecule, the oxide of Y is a simple molecule and the oxide of Z is ionic. The elements arranged in order of increasing atomic number would be

    A XYZ **B** XZY **C** YZX **D** ZXY
    E ZYX

A 3.9   Which one of the following diagrams most closely represents the shape of the phosphine molecule $PH_3(g)$?

A 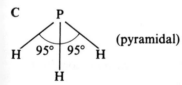 (pyramidal)

B H————P————H   (planar)
                   90° | 90°
                       H

C 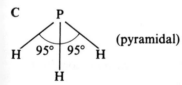 (pyramidal)

D H P H   (pyramidal)
        115° | 115°
             H

E 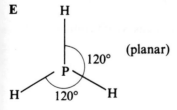 (planar)

A 3.10   Two volumes of hydrogen are mixed with five volumes of dry air at 100 °C and atmospheric pressure. The mixture is sparked so that the combustion of hydrogen goes to completion. If air contains oxygen and nitrogen in the molar ratio 1:4, what is the mole fraction of water vapour in the resulting mixture (still at 100 °C)?

A $\frac{2}{3}$ B $\frac{1}{3}$ C $\frac{2}{7}$ D $\frac{1}{4}$ E $\frac{1}{5}$

EXERCISE 4

A 4.1   Bombardment of ^{14}N with α-particles produces a hydrogen nucleus and another nucleus. This other nucleus is

A $^{14}_{6}C$ B $^{15}_{7}N$ C $^{17}_{8}O$ D $^{17}_{9}F$ E $^{18}_{10}Ne$

A 4.2   The boiling point of iodine monochloride ICl is nearly 40 °C higher than that of bromine, although the two substances have almost the same relative molecular mass. Which of the following statements best explains this observation?

A   ICl is an unsymmetrical molecule.
B   ICl has a giant covalent structure.
C   ICl is a polar molecule.
D   The I—Cl bond is stronger than the Br—Br bond.
E   The ionisation energy of iodine is lower than that of bromine.

A 4.3   A racemic mixture is defined as

A   a pair of enantiomers mixed in equal proportions.
B   a mixture of any number of optical isomers whose net optical rotation is zero.
C   an equimolar mixture of two geometrical isomers.
D   a mixture of any two optical isomers.
E   a mixture of substances which has no effect upon polarised light.

A 4.4   With how many other carbon atoms does each carbon atom in the graphite structure form a covalent bond?

A   2   B   3   C   4   D   6   E   8

A 4.5   The peaks in the mass spectrum of oxygen gas which contains ^{16}O and ^{18}O would be at mass numbers

A   17 and 34.
B   16 and 18.
C   16, 18, 32 and 36.
D   16, 18, 32, 34 and 36.
E   16, 17, 18, 32, 34 and 36.

A 4.6   The chloride ion Cl^- has the same electronic structure as

       A F^- **B** Ne   **C** Na^+ **D** Ca^{2+} **E** Al^{3+}

A 4.7   Two elements J and L have the following electronic configurations:

$$J \quad 1s^2\, 2s^2\, 2p^6\, 3s^2\, 3p^4$$
$$L \quad 1s^2\, 2s^2\, 2p^6\, 3s^2\, 3p^2$$

J and L are likely to form a compound of formula

       A JL **B** J_2L **C** JL_2 **D** J_2L_3 **E** J_3L_2

A 4.8   From a porous pot containing equimolar proportions of hydrogen and helium, the composition by mass of the mixture diffusing out is hydrogen:helium in the ratio

       A $1:1$ **B** $2:1$ **C** $4:1$ **D** $1:\sqrt{2}$ **E** $\sqrt{2}:1$

A 4.9   Ordinary hydrogen is a mixture of the isotopes ^1H and ^2H (deuterium D). In which of the following properties would the two gases hydrogen (H_2) and deuterium (D_2) differ?

1 boiling point

2 rate of diffusion under the same conditions of temperature and pressure

3 number of molecules present in a given volume at s.t.p.

A 4.10 The chemical bonding in crystalline sodium tetrahydridoborate, $NaBH_4(s)$, involves

1 ionic bonds.   **2** covalent bonds.   **3** hydrogen bonds.

SECTION B   GENERAL AND PHYSICAL CHEMISTRY II

EXERCISE 1

B 1.1   The ionic product K_w for water at 0 °C is 1.15×10^{-15} mol² dm⁻⁶ and at 60 °C is 9.6×10^{-14} mol² dm⁻⁶. From this it can be deduced that the sign of the standard enthalpy change $\Delta H^{\ominus}$ for the forward reaction

$$H_2O(l) \rightleftharpoons H^+(aq) + OH^-(aq)$$

is positive because

A   the dissociation of water is very small at both temperatures.
B   the reaction involves splitting off a proton.
C   the equilibrium is very much to the left.
D   the amount of dissociation increases with increasing temperature.
E   the dissociation of water is exothermic.

B 1.2   The diagram below relates to the reaction between carbon and hydrogen to give methane.

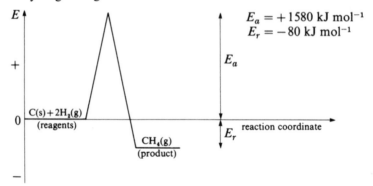

From this diagram it may be deduced that the activation energy for the reverse reaction (methane to carbon and hydrogen) would be

A $+1660$ kJ mol⁻¹   **B** $+1580$ kJ mol⁻¹   **C** $+80$ kJ mol⁻¹
D -1580 kJ mol⁻¹   **E** -1660 kJ mol⁻¹

B 1.3   The molecular conductance at infinite dilution of sodium chloride, sodium ethanoate (acetate) and hydrochloric acid are 1.26×10^{-2}, 0.91×10^{-2} and 4.26×10^{-2} Ω⁻¹ m² mol⁻¹ respectively at 25 °C. The molecular conductance at infinite dilution of ethanoic (acetic) acid at 25 °C is

A 2.09×10^{-2} Ω⁻¹ m² mol⁻¹.   **B** 3.91×10^{-2} Ω⁻¹ m² mol⁻¹.
C 4.61×10^{-2} Ω⁻¹ m² mol⁻¹.   **D** 6.43×10^{-2} Ω⁻¹ m² mol⁻¹.
E   incalculable from the values given.

B 1.4   When a mass x of a protein is dissolved in a volume V of water, the solution has an osmotic pressure of Π at an absolute (Kelvin) temperature T. If R is the gas constant, the relative molecular mass of the protein is given by

      A $\Pi V/xRT$ **B** $\Pi RV/xT$ **C** $xT/\Pi RV$
      D $RV/x\Pi T$ **E** $xRT/\Pi V$

B 1.5   Raoult's Law will be followed most closely by systems containing two liquid components A and B when

      A   there is a tendency to form a compound between A and B.
      B   one of the components tends to dimerise in the liquid phase.
      C A and B have similar physical and chemical properties.
      D   hydrogen bonding occurs between A and B.
      E   hydrogen bonding occurs extensively in one component but not in the other.

B 1.6   Which one of the following graphs would be obtained when, in a series of separate experiments, the initial rate of a first-order reaction is plotted against the initial concentration of the reactant?

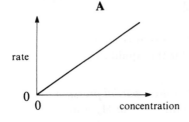

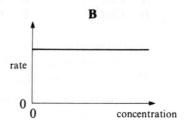

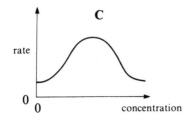

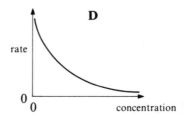

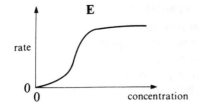

B 1.7   Which one of the following equations represents the change for which $\Delta H^{\ominus}_{298}$ would be numerically equal to the lattice energy (enthalpy) of magnesium bromide?

A $Mg^{2+}(s) + 2Br^-(s) \rightarrow MgBr_2(s)$
B $Mg^{2+}(aq) + 2Br^-(aq) \rightarrow MgBr_2(aq)$
C $Mg^{2+}(g) + 2Br^-(g) \rightarrow MgBr_2(g)$
D $Mg^{2+}(g) + 2Br^-(g) \rightarrow MgBr_2(s)$
E $Mg(g) + Br_2(g) \rightarrow MgBr_2(s)$

B 1.8   Which one of the following equations represents the process by which the standard electrode potential of an element M is defined?

A $M^{n+}(s) + ne \rightarrow M(s)$
B $M^{n+}(g) + ne \rightarrow M(g)$
C $M^{n+}(aq) + ne \rightarrow M(aq)$
D $M^{n+}(aq) + ne \rightarrow M(s)$
E $M^{n+}(g) + ne \rightarrow M(s)$

B 1.9   In which of the following compounds is the oxidation number of carbon highest?

A CH_4 B $H_2C{=}O$ C CH_2Cl_2
D $CHCl_3$ E CH_3Cl

B 1.10   Which one of the following mixtures is at equilibrium at a temperature where $K_p = 3$ atm² for the equilibrium $2NH_3(g) \rightleftharpoons N_2(g) + 3H_2(g)$?

	partial pressure of NH_3/atm	partial pressure of N_2/atm	partial pressure of H_2/atm
A	1	1.5	1
B	3	3	2
C	4	6	2
D	6	1	2
E	9	1	3

EXERCISE 2

B 2.1   An acid may generally best be regarded as

A   a proton donor or electron pair donor.
B   a proton acceptor or electron pair acceptor.
C   a proton donor or electron pair acceptor.
D   a proton acceptor or electron pair donor.
E   a substance that will turn blue litmus red.

B 2.2

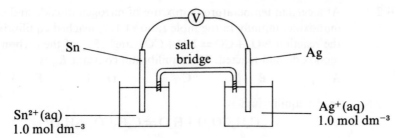

Sn — salt bridge — Ag

$Sn^{2+}(aq)$ 1.0 mol dm^{-3}

$Ag^+(aq)$ 1.0 mol dm^{-3}

Given that the standard electrode potentials for the reactions

$$Ag^+(aq) + e \rightleftharpoons Ag(s)$$

and $$Sn^{2+}(aq) + 2e \rightleftharpoons Sn(s)$$

are respectively $+0.80$ V and -0.14 V, what is the standard e.m.f. of the cell shown in the diagram above

A 0.52 V **B** 0.66 V **C** 0.87 V **D** 0.94 V
E 1.74 V

B 2.3 Ammonia forms complexes with silver(I) ions according to the following equations:

$$Ag(H_2O)_2^+(aq) + NH_3(aq) \rightleftharpoons Ag(NH_3)(H_2O)^+(aq) + H_2O(l)$$
$$Ag(NH_3)(H_2O)^+(aq) + NH_3(aq) \rightleftharpoons Ag(NH_3)_2^+(aq) + H_2O(l)$$

The equilibrium constant for the first reaction, K_1, is 2.0×10^3, and for the second reaction, K_2, it is 8.3×10^3.
What is the equilibrium constant for the following reaction?

$$Ag(H_2O)_2^+(aq) + 2NH_3(aq) \rightleftharpoons Ag(NH_3)_2^+(aq) + 2H_2O(l)$$

A 4.15 **B** 2.0×10^3 **C** 8.3×10^3 **D** 10.3×10^3
E 16.6×10^6

B 2.4 Raising the temperature of the system

$$N_2 + 3H_2 \rightleftharpoons 2NH_3 \qquad (\Delta H_{298}^{\ominus} = -44.7 \text{ kJ mol}^{-1})$$

A increases the rate of ammonia formation but has no effect on the percentage of ammonia in the equilibrium mixture.
B has no effect on the rate of ammonia formation but increases the percentage of ammonia in the equilibrium mixture.
C increases the rate of ammonia formation but decreases the percentage of ammonia in the equilibrium mixture.
D increases the rate of ammonia formation and increases the percentage of ammonia in the equilibrium mixture.
E decreases the rate of ammonia formation but increases the percentage of ammonia in the equilibrium mixture.

B 2.5   At a certain temperature, a mixture of nitrogen dioxide and carbon monoxide, initially in the mole ratio of 1:2, reached equilibrium via the reaction $NO_2 + CO \rightleftharpoons NO + CO_2$ after 25% of the carbon monoxide had reacted. The equilibrium constant K_p is

A $\frac{1}{4}$ **B** $\frac{1}{3}$ **C** $\frac{1}{2}$ **D** 1   **E** 3

B 2.6   In the equilibrium

$$C_6H_5CO_2H + H_2O \rightleftharpoons C_6H_5CO_2^- + H_3O^+$$

the equilibrium constant is most likely to be changed by

A   adding a suitable catalyst.
B   adding water.
C   adding sodium benzoate solution.
D   adding dilute sulphuric acid.
E   heating the mixture.

B 2.7   Given the following redox potentials

$$Fe^{3+}(aq)/Fe^{2+}(aq), \quad E^{\ominus} = +0.77 \text{ V}$$
$$\tfrac{1}{2}I_2(aq)/I^-(aq), \quad E^{\ominus} = +0.54 \text{ V}$$
$$\tfrac{1}{2}Cl_2(aq)/Cl^-(aq), \quad E^{\ominus} = +1.36 \text{ V}$$
$$\tfrac{1}{2}Br_2(aq)/Br^-(aq), \quad E^{\ominus} = +1.07 \text{ V}$$

which of the following statements may correctly be made?
1 $I^-(aq)$ is likely to reduce $Fe^{3+}(aq)$ to $Fe^{2+}(aq)$.
2 $Fe^{2+}(aq)$ is likely to reduce $\tfrac{1}{2}Cl_2(aq)$ to $Cl^-(aq)$.
3 $Br^-(aq)$ is likely to reduce $Fe^{3+}(aq)$ to $Fe^{2+}(aq)$.

B 2.8   Which of the following substances have a noticeable effect on the pH of water when dissolved in it?
1   potassium nitrate
2   sodium ethanoate (acetate)
3   iron(III) sulphate

B 2.9   When aqueous ammonia is added to silver chloride, the salt dissolves. Which of the following help to explain this observation?
1   The ionic product $[Ag^+ (aq)][Cl^- (aq)]$ in the solution is less than the solubility product of silver chloride.
2   A complex ion, $Ag(NH_3)_2^+$, is formed.
3   Ammonium ions and chloride ions have great affinity for each other.

B 2.10   The combustion of sodium in chlorine is an exothermic reaction. In which of the following stages of the relevant Born–Haber cycle is energy released?
1 $Na(g) \rightarrow Na^+(g) + e$
2 $Cl(g) + e \rightarrow Cl^-(g)$
3 $Na^+(g) + Cl^-(g) \rightarrow Na^+Cl^-(s)$

EXERCISE 3

B 3.1   When a small amount of an involatile solute is added to water, the
vapour pressure of the water changes. Which of the following
sketch diagrams best shows this change by means of a broken line?

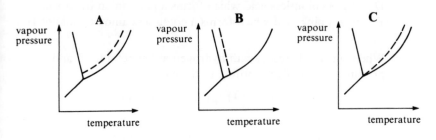

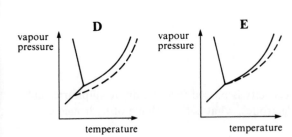

B 3.2   The rate of reaction between sulphur dioxide and oxygen to form
sulphur trioxide at 800 K can be increased by adding a
homogeneous catalyst.
Which one of the following statements about this catalyst is
correct?

A   It is a gas at 800 K.
B   It has no effect on the mechanism of reaction.
C   It increases the yield of sulphur trioxide obtained at
equilibrium.
D   It increases the activation energy for the reverse reaction.
E   It alters the enthalpy change of the reaction.

B 3.3   What is the pH of a 0.1 mol dm^{-3} solution of a fully dissociated
dibasic acid?

A   0.1   B   0.3   C   0.7   D   1.0   E   2.0

B 3.4   Phenolphthalein is pink in alkaline solutions and colourless in acid
         solutions because
         A   it is oxidised to a pink compound by OH^-.
         B   it is reduced to a pink compound by H^+.
         C   it forms a colourless cationic acid with H^+.
         D   it is a colourless acid which forms a pink anion by loss of H^+.
         E   it is a pink acid which forms a colourless anion by loss of H^+.

B 3.5   When zinc oxide reacts with hydrogen at temperature T and a
         pressure of 100 kPa according to the equation

         $$ZnO(s) + H_2(g) \rightleftharpoons Zn(g) + H_2O(g),$$

         it is found that initial amounts of 1 mol each of zinc oxide and
         hydrogen gas produce equilibrium amounts of 0.01 mol each of
         zinc and water.
         The approximate value of K_p at temperature T is
         A   100 kPa   B   10 kPa   C   1 kPa
         D 1×10^{-2} kPa   E 1×10^{-3} kPa

B 3.6   If 1 faraday of electricity is passed through dilute sulphuric acid
         using platinum electrodes, what is the volume of hydrogen evolved
         at s.t.p.?
         A   2.8 dm³   B   5.6 dm³   C   11.2 dm³   D   22.4 dm³
         E   44.8 dm³

B 3.7   One of the reasons why the solubility of lithium fluoride in water is
         less than the solubility of potassium fluoride in water is that
         A   lithium fluoride is mainly covalent.
         B   lithium fluoride has a larger enthalpy of solution than
              potassium fluoride.
         C   lithium fluoride has a larger lattice enthalpy (lattice energy)
              than potassium fluoride.
         D   lithium ions are not so heavily hydrated as potassium ions.
         E   lithium salts are not hydrolysed as much as potassium salts.

B 3.8   In the presence of an excess of dilute acid, aqueous iodine reacts with an excess of aqueous propanone (acetone) according to the equation

$$CH_3COCH_3 + I_2 \rightarrow CH_3COCH_2I + HI$$

The diagram below shows the results of plotting the concentration of iodine remaining $[I_2]$ against time from the start of the reaction.

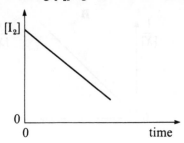

The graph shows that, under the conditions of the experiment, the rate of the reaction is

A   directly proportional to $[I_2]$.
B   inversely proportional to $[I_2]$.
C   directly proportional to $[I_2][CH_3COCH_3]$.
D   inversely proportional to $[I_2][CH_3COCH_3]$.
E   independent of $[I_2]$.

B 3.9   The ionic product of water K_w is 1.0×10^{-14} mol^2 dm^{-6} at 298 K. The neutralisation of a strong acid and a strong base is markedly exothermic. The numerical value of K_w at 273 K is likely to be

A -2.2×10^{-15} B 2.0×10^{-13} C 5.5×10^{-14}
D 1.0×10^{-14} E 1.1×10^{-15}

B 3.10   The solubility product of barium sulphate at a temperature T is 1.00×10^{-10} mol^2 dm^{-6}. The corresponding solubility of barium sulphate is

A $\dfrac{1}{2.335} \times 10^{-12}$ g dm^{-3}
B 2.335×10^{-8} g dm^{-3}
C 2.335×10^{-5} g dm^{-3}
D 2.335×10^{-3} g dm^{-3}
E 2.335×10^{7} g dm^{-3}

[The relative formula (molecular) mass of BaSO$_4$ is 233.5.]

EXERCISE 4

B 4.1   In the following graphs, $[X]$ is the concentration of a particular
reactant X at various times t for five different reactions **A, B, C, D**
and **E**. Which one of these reactions is first order with respect to
this reactant (everything else assumed present in excess)?

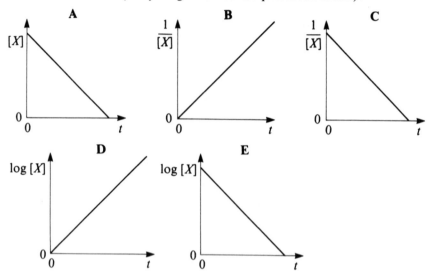

B 4.2   The figure is the phase diagram for the tin–lead system.

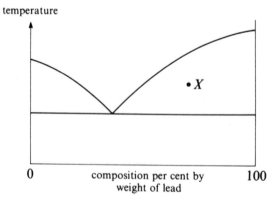

At point X the system consists of
A   solid lead and liquid of eutectic composition.
B   solid lead and liquid of composition about 50 per cent lead by
mass.
C   solid tin and solid lead.
D   solid tin and liquid of eutectic composition.
E   solid tin and liquid lead.

B 4.3   1.3 g of a metal M (relative atomic mass 52) displace 2.4 g of copper (relative atomic mass 64) from a solution of copper(II) sulphate. What is the formula of the metal ion produced in this reaction?

A M^+ B M^{2+} C M_2^{2+} D M^{3+} E M^{4+}

B 4.4   Some bond energies at 298 K are:

C—C 346 kJ mol^{-1} C=C 611 kJ mol^{-1}

C—H 413 kJ mol^{-1} H—H 437 kJ mol^{-1}

For the reaction:

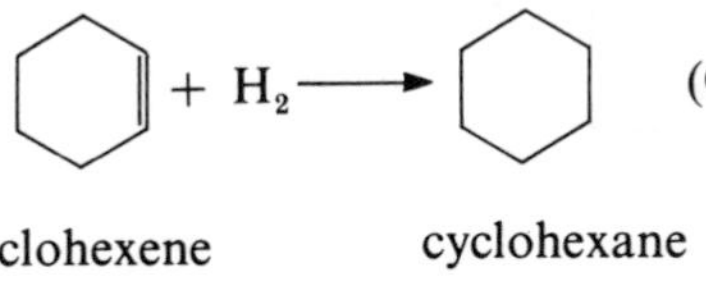

$(C_6H_{10}+H_2 \rightarrow C_6H_{12})$

cyclohexene   cyclohexane

what is the value of $\Delta H_{298}^{\ominus}$?

A -561 kJ mol^{-1}
B -124 kJ mol^{-1}
C $+124$ kJ mol^{-1}
D $+289$ kJ mol^{-1}
E $+561$ kJ mol^{-1}

B 4.5   What is the best indicator to use when titrating a solution of ammonia of concentration 0.1 mol dm^{-3} with a solution of hydrochloric acid of the same concentration? The pK_a of the ammonium ion is 9.2. [p$K_a = -\log_{10} K_a$].

A   phenolphthalein   (pH range 8 to 10)
B   phenol red   (pH range 7 to 9)
C   bromothymol blue   (pH range 6 to 8)
D   methyl red   (pH range 4 to 6)
E   bromophenol blue   (pH range 3 to 4.6)

Questions **B 4.6** *and* **B 4.7** *refer to the information below.*

The reaction between carbon monoxide and chlorine was studied by making a mixture of the two gases. At different times during the experiment, various single changes were made to the conditions inside the reaction vessel.

$$CO(g) + Cl_2(g) \rightleftharpoons COCl_2(g); \quad \Delta H = -113.4 \text{ kJ mol}^{-1}$$

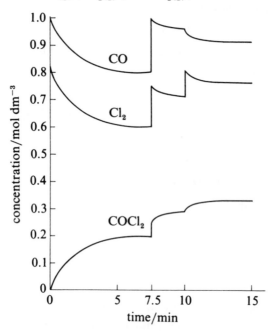

B 4.6   The changes of concentration during the period 7.5 min to 10 min could have been produced by

    A   an isothermal increase in pressure.
    B   an isothermal increase in volume.
    C   an increase in temperature.
    D   the dissociation of chlorine.
    E   the addition of chlorine and carbon monoxide to the system.

B 4.7   The changes of concentration during the period 10 min to 15 min could have been produced by

    A   an isothermal increase in pressure.
    B   an isothermal increase in volume.
    C   an increase in temperature.
    D   a decrease in temperature.
    E   the addition of more chlorine.

B 4.8   What is the pH of an aqueous solution of benzoic acid of concentration 1.0 mol dm^{-3} ($\log_{10} K_a = -4.22$)?

      A 2.11   **B** 3.22   **C** 4.22

      D 6.22   **E** some other value

B 4.9   Which of the following processes have a positive value for ΔH?

    1 $H_2(g) \rightarrow 2H(g)$

    2 $H^+(g) + e \rightarrow H(g)$

    3 $H_2O(l) \rightarrow H_2O(s)$

B 4.10   The e.m.f. of the cell $Pt \mid H_2(g), HCl(aq) \mid ZnSO_4(aq) \mid Zn$ depends on

    1 the pressure of the hydrogen.

    2 the concentration of the hydrochloric acid.

    3 the concentration of the zinc sulphate solution.

SECTION C INORGANIC CHEMISTRY

EXERCISE 1

C 1.1   The change in the oxidation state of the vanadium atom when VO^{2+} is converted into VO_2^+ is

    A -2 **B** -1 **C** 0 **D** $+1$ **E** $+2$

C 1.2   Which of the following atoms has the highest first ionisation potential?

    A lithium   **B** oxygen   **C** carbon
    D sodium   **E** fluorine

C 1.3   The element X is prepared by electrolysis of the fused chloride. It reacts with hydrogen to form a colourless solid from which hydrogen is released on addition of water. What is the element X?

    A aluminium   **B** zinc   **C** calcium
    D copper   **E** tin

C 1.4   An element X which occurs in the first short period has an outer electronic structure $s^2 p^2$. What are the formula and acid–base character of its principal oxide?

    A XO, basic   **B** XO, acidic   **C** XO_2, acidic
    D XO_2, basic   **E** X_2O_4, acidic

C 1.5   An element X reacts according to the following scheme.

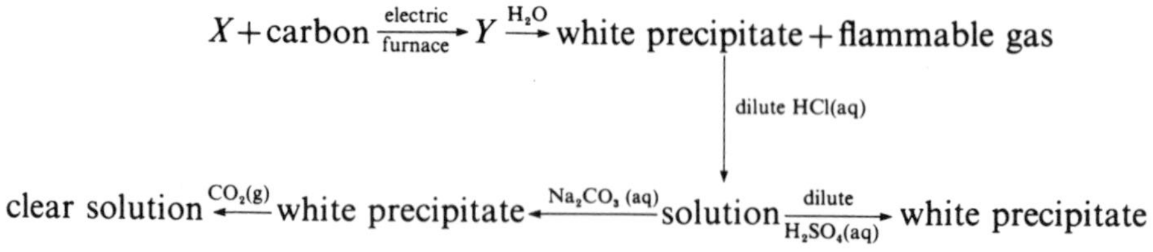

$$X + \text{carbon} \xrightarrow[\text{furnace}]{\text{electric}} Y \xrightarrow{\text{H}_2\text{O}} \text{white precipitate} + \text{flammable gas}$$

$$\downarrow \text{dilute HCl(aq)}$$

$$\text{clear solution} \xleftarrow{\text{CO}_2\text{(g)}} \text{white precipitate} \xleftarrow{\text{Na}_2\text{CO}_3 \text{ (aq)}} \text{solution} \xrightarrow[\text{H}_2\text{SO}_4\text{(aq)}]{\text{dilute}} \text{white precipitate}$$

Which one of the following elements could be X?

    A aluminium   **B** calcium   **C** magnesium
    D silicon   **E** sodium

C 1.6   When a solution of a chromium(III) salt is electrolysed the chromium is found to migrate towards the cathode. If, however, the solution is boiled with an excess of potassium cyanide and the experiment repeated, the chromium is found to migrate towards the anode. This occurs because

A   the complex $[CrCN(OH)_5]^{3-}$ is formed.
B   the complex $[Cr(OH)_4CN]^-$ is formed.
C   the complex $[Cr(CN)_4]^-$ is formed.
D   the complex $[Cr(OH)_4(CN)_2]^{3-}$ is formed.
E   the complex $[Cr(CN)_6]^{3-}$ is formed.

C 1.7   Which one of the following statements is probably correct for the halogen astatine, which lies below iodine in the Periodic Table?

A   It is a diatomic gas at normal temperature and pressure.
B   It oxidises chloride ions to chlorine.
C   It forms a hydride which undergoes considerable hydrogen bonding.
D   It undergoes simultaneous oxidation and reduction when treated with an aqueous solution of sodium hydroxide.
E   It is more electronegative than iodine.

C 1.8   How many of the elements sodium, magnesium, calcium, silicon, chromium, manganese form oxysalts in which they are present as part of the anion?

A   1   B   2   C   3   D   4   E   5

C 1.9   The enthalpy changes of formation of the gaseous oxides of nitrogen are positive. This fact is mainly due to

A   the tendency of oxygen to form oxide ions O^{2-}.
B   the high bond energy of the nitrogen molecule N_2.
C   the similarity of the electronegativities of oxygen and nitrogen.
D   the high electron affinity of oxygen atoms.
E   the high electron affinity of nitrogen atoms.

C 1.10   A piece of aluminium foil is treated with aqueous mercury(II) chloride in order to expose a clean metal surface. The foil is washed and then left to stand in water. Bubbles of gas are evolved. The final products include

A   aluminium oxide and chlorine.
B   aluminium chloride and hydrogen.
C   aluminium hydroxide and hydrogen.
D   aluminium hydroxide and oxygen.
E   aluminium hydride and oxygen.

EXERCISE 2

C 2.1   Which one of the following metals displays oxidation states of $+2$ and $+4$ in its compounds?

    A   calcium   **B**   copper   **C**   lead
    D   sodium   **E**   zinc

C 2.2   Which of the following graphs best represents the variation in the melting points of the elements sodium to chlorine?

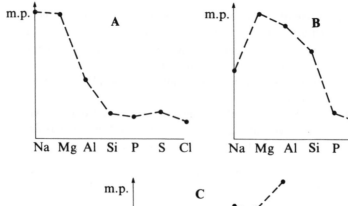

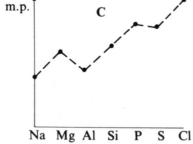

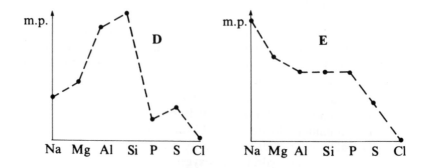

C 2.3   Which one of the following properties of the halogens and their
         compounds increases from fluorine to iodine?
         A   the bond length in the halogen molecule
         B   the electronegativity of the element
         C   the first ionisation energy of the element
         D   the lattice energy of the potassium halide
         E   the oxidising power of the element

C 2.4 X is a white powder which on heating turns yellow and gives off a
         colourless gas which has a relative vapour density of 22. The gas is
         moderately soluble in water to give a solution with a pH less than 7.
         The residue turns white on cooling and is soluble in aqueous
         solutions of sodium hydroxide, ammonia and hydrochloric acid.
         X could therefore be
         A   ammonium nitrate.
         B   manganese(II) carbonate.
         C   zinc nitrate.
         D   zinc carbonate.
         E   aluminium nitrite.

C 2.5   A solution of a metal nitrate was treated with ammonia solution
         and a brown precipitate, soluble in dilute hydrochloric acid, was
         obtained. The addition of potassium thiocyanate produced a red
         coloration. The cation was
         A $Fe^{2+}(aq)$ B $Fe^{3+}(aq)$ C $Cr^{3+}(aq)$
         D $Ag^+(aq)$ E $Pb^{2+}(aq)$

C 2.6   Which one of the following elements forms a peroxide?
         A   beryllium   B   sulphur   C   barium
         D   aluminium   E   iron

C 2.7   Which of the following compounds would be among the products
         formed when copper reacts with concentrated nitric acid?
         1   copper(I) nitrate   2   nitrogen dioxide   3   water

C 2.8   For the sequence hydrogen chloride, hydrogen bromide and
         hydrogen iodide, there is a decrease in
         1   thermal stability.   2   bond length.   3   ease of oxidation.

C 2.9   Chlorine is liberated when concentrated hydrochloric acid is
         warmed with
         1   tin(II) oxide.   2   silicon(IV) oxide.   3   lead(IV) oxide.

C 2.10   A solid dissolved without the evolution of any gas on being warmed with an excess of aqueous sodium hydroxide. A colourless solution was left. Which of the following salts have these properties?

   1 lead(II) nitrate   **2** sodium nitrite   **3** ammonium nitrate

EXERCISE 3

C 3.1   A white crystalline solid reacts with dilute hydrochloric acid to give a pale yellow precipitate and a colourless gas that decolourises aqueous bromine. The solid is most likely to be
   A sodium carbonate.
   B sodium sulphate.
   C sodium sulphide.
   D sodium sulphite.
   E sodium thiosulphate.

C 3.2   In which one of the following ways is the chemistry of beryllium *typical* of that of the elements in Group II of the Periodic Table?
   A Beryllium does not react with steam.
   B Beryllium oxide is amphoteric.
   C Beryllium chloride is covalent.
   D Beryllium nitride evolves ammonia on contact with water.
   E Beryllium forms complex ions such as BeF_4^{2-}.

C 3.3   Which of the following elements in the second short period has the highest boiling point?
   A sodium   **B** magnesium   **C** aluminium
   D phosphorus   **E** sulphur

C 3.4   An element X is a solid at room temperature, its melting point is approximately 450 °C and it is a non-conductor of electricity. 1 mol of X atoms combines with 2 mol of chlorine atoms to form a chloride that is readily hydrolysed in water. To which one of the following groups of the Periodic Table is X most likely to belong?
   A Group II   **B** Group III   **C** Group VI
   D Group VII   **E** *d*-block

C 3.5   Which one of the following mixtures evolves the greatest volume of ammonia (measured at s.t.p.) when boiled with an excess of aqueous sodium hydroxide?

A   1 mol of CH_3NH_2 and 1 mol of NH_4Cl
B   1 mol of $C_6H_5NH_2$ and 1 mol of NH_4Cl
C   1 mol of $C_6H_5NH_3^+Cl^-$ and 1 mol of NH_4Cl
D   1 mol of $CH_3CO_2NH_4$ and 1 mol of $(NH_4)_2SO_4$
E   1 mol of $C_6H_5NH_3^+Cl^-$ and 1 mol of $(NH_4)_2SO_4$

C 3.6   Which one of the following reagents would completely dissolve an alloy of copper and zinc?

A   dilute hydrochloric acid
B   dilute nitric acid
C   dilute sulphuric acid
D   aqueous sodium hydroxide
E   aqueous sodium carbonate

C 3.7   An oxide of lead is prepared by heating lead in air at 500 °C followed by treatment with cold concentrated nitric acid. The oxide left has the formula

A PbO B Pb_3O_4 C Pb_2O_3 D PbO_2 E PbO_4

C 3.8   When 10.0 cm³ of a 0.10 mol dm⁻³ solution of an alkali metal salt MXO_3 was reduced with an excess of acidified potassium iodide solution, the resulting iodine required 60.0 cm³ of 0.10 mol dm⁻³ sodium thiosulphate solution for its reduction. The anion could have been reduced to

A XO_2 B XO_2^- C XO^- D XO E X^-

C 3.9   A solution containing one of the following metal ions gave a white precipitate when aqueous sodium carbonate was added. After being filtered off, washed and dried, the precipitate did not give carbon dioxide when treated with acid. Which metal ion was present initially?

A Al^{3+} (aq)   B Fe^{3+} (aq)   C Mg^{2+} (aq)
D Pb^{2+} (aq)   E Zn^{2+} (aq)

C 3.10   An aqueous solution of a cation X^{n+} was found to give (a) a dark brown precipitate with hydrogen sulphide in acid solution, (b) free iodine with aqueous iodide ions, and (c) a metallic deposit when treated with granulated zinc. X^{n+} was therefore

A Pb^{4+} B Fe^{3+} C Sn^{4+} D Cr^{3+} E Cu^{2+}

EXERCISE 4

C 4.1   When the salt $Et_4N^+Cl^-$ is treated with gaseous hydrogen chloride, a white solid X is formed. When X is dissolved in water, a 20 cm^3 portion of the solution requires 24.6 cm^3 of aqueous NaOH of concentration 0.1 mol dm^{-3} for neutralisation; a further 20 cm^3 portion of the solution requires 49.2 cm^3 of $AgNO_3$ of concentration 0.1 mol dm^{-3} for complete precipitation of the chloride as AgCl. The formula of the anion present in X is

   A $H_2Cl_3^-$ B HCl_2^- C HCl_3^{2-} D HCl_4^{3-}
   E $H_2Cl_6^{4-}$

C 4.2   Hydrogen behaves as an oxidising agent when it reacts
   A   with calcium to give calcium hydride.
   B   with bromine to given hydrogen bromide.
   C   with nitrogen to give ammonia.
   D   with sulphur to give hydrogen sulphide.
   E   with ethene (ethylene) to give ethane.

C 4.3   An element X yielded a white crystalline solid when it was heated in a stream of dry hydrogen. On treatment with water, this white solid yielded a quarter of its own mass of hydrogen. The element X is

   A   sodium.   B   aluminium.   C   beryllium.
   D   lithium.   E   carbon.
   [Relative atomic masses: Li, 7; Be, 9; C, 12; Na, 23; Al, 27.]

C 4.4   An element M with an atomic number of less than 10 forms (a) a chloride which hydrolyses rapidly, and (b) a gaseous hydride which reacts vigorously with oxygen to form a solid oxide. What is the formula of the oxide?

   A M_2O B M_2O_3 C MO_2 D M_2O_2 E M_2O_4

C 4.5   Which one of the following statements about elements in Group V of the Periodic Table is *correct*? With increasing atomic number of X,
   A   the electrical conductivity of the solid element X increases.
   B   the oxides X_2O_3 become increasingly acidic.
   C   the hydrides XH_3 display increasing thermal stability.
   D   the chlorides XCl_3 display an increasingly covalent nature.
   E   the higher oxidation state (valency) of X is formed with increasing ease.

C 4.6 In the same Period, atomic volumes are greatest for elements of Group
A I (the alkali metals)
B II (the alkaline earths)
C IV (carbon–lead)
D V (nitrogen–bismuth)
E VII (the halogens)

C 4.7 Rhodium is a metal in the second transition series. Which of the following properties are likely to be important features of its chemistry?
1 formation of complexes with a wide variety of ligands
2 formation of a peroxide on heating in oxygen
3 formation of an ionic hydride RhH_2

C 4.8 Which of the following properties of the Group IV elements, carbon to lead, increase with increasing atomic number?
1 the stability of compounds in which the oxidation state of the Group IV element is $+2$
2 the first ionisation energy
3 the stability of the tetrahydride

C 4.9 In the presence of an excess of cyanide ions in aqueous solution, Fe(II) is not oxidised to Fe(III) by atmospheric oxygen because
1 the redox potential of the Fe(III)/Fe(II) system is altered by complexing with cyanide ions.
2 the redox potential of the O_2/OH^- system is altered by the presence of cyanide ions.
3 oxygen preferentially oxidises the cyanide ions.

C 4.10 When a mixture of two gases is sparked, an explosion occurs. Which of the following mixtures would show this behaviour?
1 H_2 and O_2 2 H_2 and Cl_2 3 H_2 and N_2

SECTION D ORGANIC CHEMISTRY

EXERCISE 1

D 1.1 The oxidation of propan-2-ol, $CH_3CH(OH)CH_3$, by sodium
dichromate(VI) leads to the formation of
A   propanone (CH_3COCH_3).
B   propan-1-ol ($CH_3CH_2CH_2OH$).
C   propanoic acid ($CH_3CH_2CO_2H$).
D   propanal (CH_3CH_2CHO).
E   methoxyethane ($CH_3OCH_2CH_3$).

D 1.2 Which one of the following pairs of substances would react to give
methyl benzoate $C_6H_5CO_2CH_3$?
A   ethanoic (acetic) acid and phenol
B   ethanoic acid and phenylmethanol (benzyl alcohol)
C   benzoic acid and ethanol
D   benzoyl chloride and sodium phenoxide (phenate)
E   benzoic acid and methanol

D 1.3 Which one of the following pairs of compounds could, in theory,
produce a polyamide if heated together under suitable conditions?
A   a monocarboxylic acid and a mono-amine
B   a monocarboxylic acid and a diamine
C   a monocarboxylic acid and ammonia
D   a dicarboxylic acid and a mono-amine
E   a dicarboxylic acid and a diamine

D 1.4 Benzene was added gradually to a mixture of concentrated nitric
acid and concentrated sulphuric acid and the temperature was not
allowed to exceed 60 °C. The mixture was then poured into water.
The chief component of the oily layer which separated was

A $C_6H_5SO_3H$ B $C_6H_5NO_2$ C $C_6H_5NO_3$

D   E

D 1.5   The relative reactivity of propene (propylene) and ethanal (acetaldehyde) towards attack by cyanide ion can be explained in terms of the general principle that

     A   nucleophiles attack a C=O carbon atom more readily than a C=C carbon atom.

     B   electrophiles attack a C=O carbon atom more readily than a C=C carbon atom.

     C   both nucleophiles and electrophiles attack a C=O carbon atom more readily than a C=C carbon atom.

     D   nucleophiles attack a C=C carbon atom more readily than a C=O carbon atom.

     E   electrophiles attack a C=C carbon atom more readily than a C=O carbon atom.

D 1.6   A substance X, $C_2H_2Cl_2O$, reacts with cold water to give an acid $C_2H_3ClO_2$, and this is converted slowly by hot water into another acid $C_2H_4O_3$. What is X?

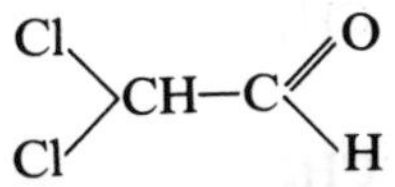

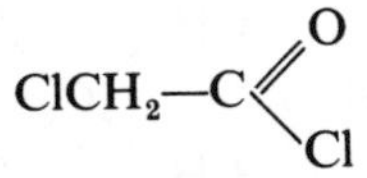

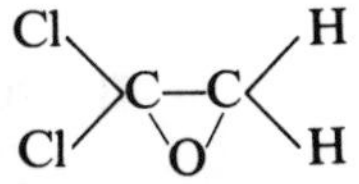

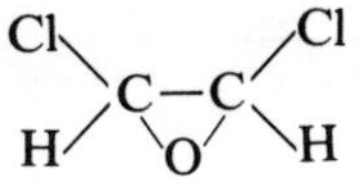

D 1.7   One mole of an organic compound of molecular formula C_6H_8 was found to react, in the presence of a suitable catalyst, with two moles of hydrogen. Which one of the formulae below is consistent with these data?

     A $CH_2{=}CH{-}CH_2{-}CH_2{-}CH{=}CH_2$

     B $CH_2{=}CH{-}CH{=}CH{-}CH{=}CH_2$

     C $CH_2{=}CH{-}C{\equiv}C{-}CH_2{-}CH_3$

     D

     E

D 1.8   Which one of the following reagents would be the most suitable for carrying out the conversion below?

$$CH_3-\langle\bigcirc\rangle-N_2^+Cl^- \longrightarrow CH_3-\langle\bigcirc\rangle-Cl$$

A   chlorine gas in sunlight
B   chlorine gas and a halogen carrier
C   dilute hydrochloric acid
D   copper(I) chloride and hydrochloric acid
E   phosphorus pentachloride

D 1.9   Which one of the following equations correctly represents the aldol reaction, involving propanone (acetone)?

A $2CH_3CCH_3 \rightarrow CH_3CCH_2CH_2CCH_3$
       $\quad\quad\;\; \overset{\|}{O} \quad\quad\quad\; \overset{\|}{O} \quad\quad\; \overset{\|}{O}$

B $2CH_3CCH_3 \rightarrow$
       $\quad\quad\;\; \overset{\|}{O}$

C $2CH_3CCH_3 \rightarrow HO{>}C{-}C{<}OH$
       $\quad\quad\;\; \overset{\|}{O}$

D $2CH_3CCH_3 \rightarrow HO{>}CCH_2CCH_3$
       $\quad\quad\;\; \overset{\|}{O}$

E $2CH_3CCH_3 \rightarrow$
       $\quad\quad\;\; \overset{\|}{O}$

D 1.10   How many isomers of molecular formula C_8H_{10} contain a benzene ring?

    A   1   B   2   C   3   D   4   E   5

EXERCISE 2

D 2.1   When benzene is nitrated by using a mixture of concentrated nitric acid and concentrated sulphuric acid, what is the species initially attacking the benzene molecule?

A NO_3^- B NO_2^+ C NO_2^- D HNO_3 E HSO_4^-

D 2.2   In which one of the following molecules would the carbon–halogen bond be most readily broken by aqueous alkali?

A $ClCH_2CO_2H$ B $HCCl_3$ C C_6H_5Cl
D CCl_4 E CH_3COCl

D 2.3   Which one of the following compounds is most likely to act as a monomer in an addition polymerisation process?

A $HOCH_2CH_2C\overset{\displaystyle O}{\underset{\displaystyle OH}{<}}$

B $CH_3CH_2CH_2NH_2$

C $CH_3CH_2C\overset{\displaystyle O}{\underset{\displaystyle OH}{<}}$

D $CH_3CH_2C\overset{\displaystyle O}{\underset{\displaystyle Cl}{<}}$

E $CH_3CH=CH_2$

D 2.4   What is the main product when a mixture of ethanol and a large excess of concentrated sulphuric acid is heated to 160–170 °C?

A   ethane
B   ethyne (acetylene)
C   ethoxyethane (diethyl ether)
D   ethene (ethylene)
E   ethyl hydrogensulphate

D 2.5   Methanol and ethanol may easily be distinguished from one another by their reaction with

A   sodium.
B   phosphorus pentachloride.
C   alkaline sodium iodate(I) (hypoiodite) solution.
D   hydrogen chloride.
E   ethanoic (acetic) acid.

D 2.6   Which one of the following esters is obtained by the esterification of propan-2-ol with ethanoic (acetic) acid?
   A $(CH_3)_2CHCO_2CH_3$
   B $CH_3CO_2CH_2CH_3$
   C $CH_3CH_2CO_2CH(CH_3)_2$
   D $(CH_3)_2CHCO_2CH_2CH_3$
   E $CH_3CO_2CH(CH_3)_2$

D 2.7   Which of the following compounds yield *more than one* monobromo substitution product?
   1   ethane   2   dimethylpropane   3   propane

D 2.8   Which of the following reagents are suitable for converting a carboxylic acid into an acyl (acid) chloride?
   1   hydrogen chloride
   2   chlorine
   3   phosphorus pentachloride

D 2.9   When ethene (ethylene) is passed into bromine to make 1,2-dibromoethane, the reaction may become too vigorous. Which of the following might be used to slow the reaction down?
   1   surrounding the reaction vessel with cold water
   2   dissolving the bromine in an inert solvent
   3   adding the ethene more slowly

D 2.10   Which of the following compounds, when dissolved in water, give a neutral solution?
   1   $C_2H_5NH_2$ 2 CH_3COCH_3 3 C_2H_5OH

EXERCISE 3

D 3.1   When ethene (ethylene) is bubbled into an aqueous solution containing bromine and sodium chloride, it is possible to isolate some CH_2BrCH_2Br and some CH_2BrCH_2Cl but no CH_2ClCH_2Cl. The simplest interpretation of these results involves which one of the following intermediates?
   A $ClCH_2CH_2^+$ B $HOCH_2CH_2^-$ C $BrCH_2CH_2^-$
   D $BrCH_2CH_2^+$ E $HOCH_2CH_2^+$

D 3.2   How many different substitution products are, in principle, possible when a mixture of bromine and ethane are allowed to react?
   A   1   B   3   C   5   D   7   E   9

D 3.3   The rate of the reaction $RBr + OH^- \longrightarrow$ products (where
$R = (CH_3)_3C-$) was found to be directly proportional to the
concentration of RBr and independent of the concentration of
hydroxide ions, i.e. rate $= k[RBr]$.
Which one of the following reaction mechanisms best fits these
results?

A $RBr + OH^- \xrightarrow{\text{slow}} RBrOH^-$

$RBrOH^- \xrightarrow{\text{fast}} ROH + Br^-$

B $RBr \xrightarrow{\text{fast}} R^+ + Br^-$

$R^+ + OH^- \xrightarrow{\text{slow}} ROH$

C $RBr \xrightarrow{\text{slow}} R^+ + Br^-$

$R^+ + OH^- \xrightarrow{\text{fast}} ROH$

D $RBr + OH^- \xrightarrow{\text{fast}} RBrOH^-$

$RBrOH^- \xrightarrow{\text{slow}} ROH + Br^-$

E $RBr + OH^- \xrightarrow{\text{slow}} HOBr + R^-$

$R^- + HOBr \xrightarrow{\text{fast}} ROH + Br^-$

D 3.4   The order of increasing acid strength (weakest first) of the four acids

I. $CH_3CH_2CH_2CO_2H$
II. $CH_2ClCH_2CH_2CO_2H$
III. $CH_3CH_2CHClCO_2H$
IV. $CH_3CH_2CCl_2CO_2H$

may be deduced to be

A   I, II, III, IV   B   I, IV, III, II   C   II, III, IV, I
D   IV, III, I, II   E   IV, III, II, I

D 3.5   Geraniol can be isolated from oil of geranium and has the
following structure:

$(CH_3)_2C{=}CHCH_2CH_2C(CH_3){=}CHCH_2OH.$

It would be expected to

A   give a purple colour with a solution of iron(III) chloride.
B   produce an alkane on reaction with hydrogen, using a nickel
catalyst.
C   reduce Fehling's solution.
D   decolourise a solution of bromine in tetrachloromethane
(carbon tetrachloride).
E   dissolve in aqueous sodium hydroxide, forming a sodium salt.

D 3.6   An organic compound gave the following reactions:
(i) when heated strongly in air, a white residue remained;
(ii) when warmed with ethanol and concentrated sulphuric acid, an ester was produced.
The original compound could have been

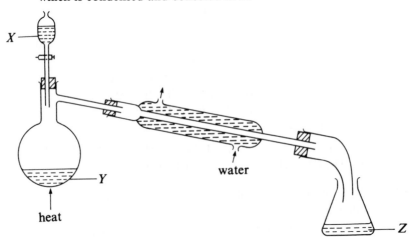

D 3.7   2.8 g of a pure alkene containing only one double bond per molecule react completely with 8.0 g of bromine in an inert solvent. What is the molecular formula of the alkene?

A C_2H_4 B C_3H_6 C C_4H_8 D C_6H_{12} E C_8H_{16}

D 3.8   In the apparatus in the diagram below, when the reagent X is added to the heated flask containing the reagent Y, a vapour is given off which is condensed and collected at Z.

Which one of the following combinations is correct?

	X	Y	Z
A	acidified $K_2Cr_2O_7$	C_2H_5OH	CH_3CHO
B	alkaline $KMnO_4$	C_2H_5OH	CH_3CO_2H
C	CH_3CO_2H	C_2H_5OH	$CH_3CO_2C_2H_5$
D	concentrated HNO_3	C_6H_6	$C_6H_5NO_2$
E	alkaline $KMnO_4$	$C_6H_5CH_3$	$C_6H_5CO_2H$

D 3.9   The product (sodium ethoxide) of dissolving sodium in ethanol is

   A   a non-ionic solid.   **B**   a strong base.   **C**   a weak base.
   D   a strong acid.   **E**   a weak acid.

D 3.10   It is known that the deuterium analogue of benzene, C_6D_6, is nitrated at the same rate as ordinary benzene. When C_6H_5D is nitrated, four mononitration products may be isolated:

   I   II   III   IV

Which one of the following shows the mole ratio in which these four products would be obtained?

	I	II	III	IV
A	1	1	1	1
B	1	2	2	2
C	2	1	1	1
D	2	1	1	2
E	1	2	2	1

EXERCISE 4

D 4.1   When ethyl ethanoate, $CH_3C^{16}O_2C_2H_5$, undergoes acid hydrolysis in the presence of $H_2^{18}O$, atoms of the ^{18}O isotope appear in the product as $CH_3-C{<}^{18}OH_{,O}$ and not as $C_2H_5^{18}OH$. Which one of the following statements may be *deduced* from this observation?

   A   A $C-^{16}O$ bond is stronger than a $C-^{18}O$ bond.
   B   The O–C bond of the $O-C_2H_5$ group of the ester is broken during the hydrolysis.
   C   The carbon–oxygen single bond of the $-\overset{O}{\underset{||}{C}}-O$ group of the ester is broken.
   D   The oxygen atom of the OC_2H_5 group undergoes attack by $H_3^{18}O^+$.
   E   The C_2H_5 group undergoes attack by $H_2^{18}O$.

D 4.2   If an equimolar mixture of $CH_2{=}CHC{\equiv}N$, propenonitrile (acrylonitrile), and $CH_2{=}CHCl$, chloroethene (vinyl chloride), undergoes addition polymerisation the polymer is likely to contain units of

A $-CH_2-CHCl-CH_2-CH-$
$\qquad\qquad\qquad\qquad\ \ |$
$\qquad\qquad\qquad\qquad\ \ C{\equiv}N$

B $-CH_2-CHCl-C{=}N-$
$\qquad\qquad\qquad\ |$
$\qquad\qquad\qquad\ CH{=}CH_2$

C $-CH_2-CH{=}C{=}N-CH_2-CHCl-$

D $-CH_2-CH{=}CH-CH-$
$\qquad\qquad\qquad\qquad\ |$
$\qquad\qquad\qquad\qquad\ C{\equiv}N$

E $-CH{=}CCl-CH_2-CH{=}CH-NH-$

D 4.3   If ethanoic (acetic) acid was dissolved in a large excess of D_2O, how many hydrogen atoms in the acid molecule would rapidly be replaced by deuterium atoms?
A none **B** 1 **C** 2 **D** 3 **E** 4

D 4.4   A general method for separating benzene from a mixture of benzene and an organic amine could involve
A   adding ethanol to the mixture.
B   burning off the benzene.
C   shaking the mixture with dilute aqueous acid.
D   shaking the mixture with dilute aqueous alkali.
E   nitrating the benzene with a nitrating mixture.

D 4.5   Which one of the following species attacks butane C_4H_{10}?
A   sodium atoms
B   sodium ions
C   chloride ions
D   chlorine atoms
E   chlorine molecules

D 4.6   Which one of the following statements about the ability of the
compound $C_6H_5COCH_2Br$ to undergo the haloform reaction is
correct?

A   The reaction will proceed because the CO—C bond breaks in
the first step, which is followed by halogenation of the two
C—H bonds.

B   The reaction will proceed because halogenation of the two
C—H bonds can take place readily, and is followed by CO—C
bond breaking.

C   The reaction will not proceed because the halogen attacks the
CH_2Br group first.

D   The reaction will not proceed because $C_6H_4COCH_2Br$ does not
contain a $COCH_3$ grouping.

E   The reaction will not proceed because the CO—C bond breaks
first under the conditions employed for a haloform reaction.

D 4.7   Reaction of ethanol with sulphuric acid under suitable conditions
can lead to the formation of

1   ethyl hydrogensulphate.
2   ethoxyethane (diethyl ether).
3   ethene (ethylene).

D 4.8   Which of the following statements about benzene are true?

1   The molecule is planar.
2   There are two different C—C bond distances in the molecule,
corresponding to alternate single and double bonds.
3   It has an unusually low delocalisation energy.

D 4.9   Which of the following reactions take place very rapidly?

1   the hydrolysis of a nitrile, R—C≡N, by water
2   the reaction between trichloromethane (chloroform) and silver
nitrate solution
3   the hydrolysis of ethanoyl (acetyl) chloride by water

D 4.10   Which of the following statements concerning phenylamine (aniline)
are true?

1   It is a weaker base than methylamine.
2   It reacts with ethanoyl (acetyl) chloride to give an amide.
3   It yields nitrogen when treated with nitrous acid at a
temperature of 0 °C.

SECTION E GENERAL AND PHYSICAL CHEMISTRY I AND II

EXERCISE 1

E 1.1 The diagram below shows a radioactive source in a lead block which is emitting mixed α, β, γ radiation through an electric field towards a photographic plate.

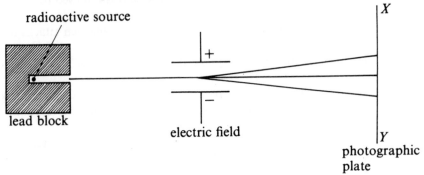

Which one of the following arrangements would be produced on the photographic plate?

	A		B		C		D		E
	X		X		X		X		X
β	•	α	•	β	•	γ	•	α	•
α	•	γ	•	γ	•	α	•	β	•
γ	•	β	•	α	•	β	•	γ	•
	Y		Y		Y		Y		Y

E 1.2 Which of the following statements *best* explains the action of a catalyst in speeding up a chemical reaction?

A   It prevents the back reaction from occurring.
B   It increases the kinetic energy of the reacting molecules.
C   It makes the enthalpy change ΔH for the reaction more negative.
D   It increases the equilibrium constant for the reaction.
E   It lowers the energy barrier for the reaction.

E 1.3   Which one of the following molecules is chiral?

A $O=S\diagdown^{Cl}_{Cl}$

B   HO—⬡—Cl

C $Cl-\underset{\underset{Cl}{|}}{\overset{\overset{Cl}{|}}{Si}}-Cl$

D $CH_3-\underset{\underset{NH_3}{|}}{\overset{\overset{H}{|}}{C}}-CO_2H$

E $\underset{Cl}{\overset{H}{\diagdown}}C=C\underset{Cl}{\overset{H}{\diagup}}$

E 1.4   Consider the solubility curves given in the diagram below.

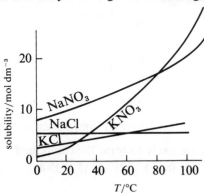

What is the chemical nature of the first crystals which separate when a solution containing equal concentrations of NaCl and KNO_3 is evaporated by boiling under a pressure of 1 atmosphere?

A   NaCl   B   KCl   C $NaNO_3$
D KNO_3 E $NaCl+KNO_3$

E 1.5   A pure substance may exist in three phases, solid, liquid or gas, under specified conditions of temperature and pressure. Which one of the following statements is correct?

A   All phases can exist together under all conditions.
B   Two phases can exist together under all conditions.
C   One phase only can exist under all conditions.
D   All phases can exist together under a limited range of conditions.
E   Two phases can exist together under a limited range of conditions.

E 1.6   At room temperature caesium chloride and sodium chloride do not have the same type of crystal lattice. The explanation given for the formation of different structures is that caesium and sodium have different

A   ionic radii.
B   ionic charges.
C   ionisation potentials.
D   covalent radii.
E   co-ordination numbers.

E 1.7   If α is the degree of dissociation of a solution of ethanoic (acetic) acid of concentration C, the dissociation constant, K_a, is given by

A $\dfrac{(1-\alpha)}{\alpha^2 C}$ **B** $\dfrac{(1-\alpha)^2}{\alpha C}$ **C** $\dfrac{\alpha}{C(1-\alpha)^2}$

D $\dfrac{\alpha^2 C}{(1-\alpha)}$ **E** $\dfrac{\alpha C}{(1-\alpha)^2}$

E 1.8   Two atoms X and Y with the electron configurations

$$1s^2\,2s^2\,2p^6\,3s^2 \text{ and } 1s^2\,2s^2\,2p^6\,3s^2\,2p^4$$

respectively are likely to form the compound

A X^+Y^- **B** $X^{2+}Y^{2-}$ **C** $X{-}Y$ **D** $X{=}Y$
E $X_2\,Y_2$

E 1.9   A vessel contains a mixture of one volume of oxygen and two volumes of hydrogen. The hydrogen and oxygen will have the same

A   partial pressures.
B   number of molecules in the mixture.
C   mean kinetic energies of their molecules.
D   root mean square velocities of their molecules.
E   rate of diffusion or effusion.

E 1.10   The data below refer to gas phase reactions at constant pressure.

$$CH_3{-}CH_3 \rightarrow CH_3{-}CH_2^{\cdot} + H^{\cdot}\ ;\ \Delta H^{\ominus} = +412 \text{ kJ mol}^{-1}:$$
$$CH_3{-}CH_2^{\cdot} \rightarrow CH_2{=}CH_2 + H^{\cdot}\ ;\ \Delta H^{\ominus} = +168 \text{ kJ mol}^{-1}.$$

Using these data, what is the enthalpy change $\Delta H^{\ominus}$ for the following reaction?

$$2\,CH_3{-}CH_2^{\cdot} \rightarrow CH_3{-}CH_3 + CH_2{=}CH_2$$

A -580 kJ mol^{-1} **B** -244 kJ mol^{-1} **C** -122 kJ mol^{-1}
D $+244$ kJ mol^{-1} **E** $+580$ kJ mol^{-1}

EXERCISE 2

E 2.1

Substance	Standard enthalpy (heat) of combustion/kJ mol⁻¹
Hydrogen (g)	-300
Carbon (s)	-400
Benzene (l)	-3300

By using the data in the above table, what is the standard enthalpy change of formation of liquid benzene?

A -4000 kJ mol⁻¹   B -800 kJ mol⁻¹   C   0 kJ mol⁻¹
D $+500$ kJ mol⁻¹   E $+1200$ kJ mol⁻¹

E 2.2   The following equilibrium may be set up in the gas phase.

$$2NO(g) + Cl_2(g) \rightleftharpoons 2NOCl(g)$$

In what units, if any, would the equilibrium constant K_c be measured?

A   mol dm⁻³
B   mol² dm⁻⁶
C   dm³ mol⁻¹
D   dm⁶ mol⁻²
E   The constant would have no units.

E 2.3   The same current was passed through molten sodium chloride and through molten cryolite containing aluminium oxide. If 4.6 g of sodium were liberated in one cell, the mass of aluminium liberated in the other cell was

A   0.9 g   B   1.8 g   C   2.7 g   D   3.6 g   E   5.4 g
[Relative atomic masses: Na, 23; Al, 27.]

E 2.4   The hydrolysis of sucrose in aqueous solution is catalysed by hydrogen ions, e.g. from hydrochloric acid. To determine the order of this reaction with respect to hydrogen ions, you should

A   measure the change in pH during the reaction.
B   remove samples at various time intervals and titrate against a standard solution of sodium hydroxide.
C   add a suitable indicator and watch for the time when the colour changes.
D   measure the rate of the reaction several times, but with a different concentration of sucrose each time.
E   measure the rate of the reaction several times, but with a different concentration of hydrochloric acid each time.

E 2.5   Diamond is an insulator because

    A   it is crystalline.
    B   it contains too few electrons.
    C   its electrons are delocalised.
    D   its atoms are widely spaced.
    E   it has single covalent bonds only.

E 2.6   Which one of the following correctly represents the orbital distribution of the electrons in the sulphide anion?

    A $1s^2\ 2s^2\ 2p^4$
    B $1s^2\ 2s^2\ 2p^6$
    C $1s^2\ 2s^2\ 2p^6\ 3s^2\ 3p^2$
    D $1s^2\ 2s^2\ 2p^6\ 3s^2\ 3p^4$
    E $1s^2\ 2s^2\ 2p^6\ 3s^2\ 3p^6$

E 2.7   What is the approximate O—C—O bond angle in ethyl ethanoate (acetate)?

    A   90°   **B**   104.5°   **C**   109°   **D**   120°   **E**   180°

E 2.8   On repeated sparking, 10 cm³ of a mixture of carbon monoxide and nitrogen required 3 cm³ oxygen for combustion. What was the volume of nitrogen in the mixture? [All volumes were measured at room temperature and pressure.]

    A $3\tfrac{1}{3}$ cm³   **B**   4 cm³   **C**   5 cm³   **D**   7 cm³   **E** $8\tfrac{1}{2}$ cm³

E 2.9   The shape of the methyl cation (CH_3^+) is likely to be

    A   linear.   **B**   planar.   **C**   tetrahedral.
    D   spherical.   **E**   pyramidal.

E 2.10   When calcium carbonate is heated in a closed vessel, it dissociates into calcium oxide and carbon dioxide:

$$CaCO_3(s) \rightleftharpoons CaO(s) + CO_2(g)$$

The equilibrium constant for this reaction is given by

    A $K = p\,CO_2$

    B $K = \dfrac{\text{(moles of } CaCO_3)}{\text{(moles of } CaO)\ \text{(moles of } CO_2)}$

    C $K = \dfrac{\text{(moles of } CaO)\ \text{(moles of } CO_2)}{\text{(moles of } CaCO_3)}$

    D $K = \dfrac{(p\,CaO)\ (p\,CO_2)}{(p\,CaCO_3)}$

    E $K = \dfrac{(p\,CaCO_3)}{(p\,CO_2)\ (p\,CaO)}$

[p = partial pressure]

EXERCISE 3

E 3.1 Which of the following statements best illustrates a major characteristic of elements having an outer electron shell containing five p electrons?

    A They commonly exhibit variable valency and solutions of their ions are usually strongly coloured.

    B They are the most strongly electronegative elements.

    C They are generally solids at room temperature.

    D They have low ionisation potentials.

    E They form predominantly ionically bonded compounds.

E 3.2 What are the units in which the solubility product of calcium phosphate(v), $Ca_3(PO_4)_2$, is expressed?

    A $mol\ dm^{-3}$ **B** $mol^2\ dm^{-6}$ **C** $mol^3\ dm^{-9}$

    D $mol^4\ dm^{-12}$ **E** $mol^5\ dm^{-15}$

E 3.3 The enthalpies of formation of ethyne (acetylene) and benzene (gas) at 25 °C are 230 and 85 kJ mol^{-1} respectively. The enthalpy change, ΔH, for the reaction $3C_2H_2(g) \rightarrow C_6H_6(g)$ at 25 °C is

    A 145 kJ mol^{-1} **B** -605 kJ mol^{-1}

    C -145 kJ mol^{-1} **D** 605 kJ mol^{-1}

    E impossible to work out because benzene is a liquid at 25 °C

E 3.4 When a certain solution of a weak acid X is titrated with a solution of a strong base Y the pH of the solution varies as shown below

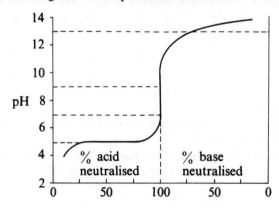

A good buffer solution may be made from mixtures of the solutions X and Y to have an appoximate pH of

    A 5 only   **B** 9 only   **C** either 5 or 13

    D between 5 and 13   **E** 7 only

E 3.5 α (rhombic) sulphur is stable below 95.6 °C and β (monoclinic) sulphur above 95.6 °C. This statement implies that

A α and β sulphur exhibit dynamic allotropy.
B α and β sulphur are monotropes.
C α and β sulphur are enantiotropes.
D   the vapour pressure of α sulphur is always greater than that of β sulphur.
E   95.6 °C is the critical temperature.

E 3.6   Two gases, X and Y, react according to the overall equation: $X(g) + 3Y(g) \rightarrow XY_3(g)$. In an attempt to determine the rate equation for the reaction, the following results were obtained at 350 K.

Experiment	$[X]$/mol dm^{-3}	$[Y]$/mol dm^{-3}	Corresponding rate of formation of XY_3/ mol dm^{-3} min^{-1}
1	0.10	0.10	0.002
2	0.10	0.20	0.008
3	0.10	0.30	0.018
4	0.20	0.10	0.002
5	0.30	0.10	0.002

The rate of the reaction is given by the expression

A $k[X][Y]^3$ **B** $k[X][Y]^2$ **C** $k[Y]^2$
D $k[X][Y]$ **E** $k[Y]^3$

E 3.7   The number of non-cyclic isomers of molecular formula C_3H_5Br is
A 1   **B** 2   **C** 3   **D** 4   **E** 5

E 3.8   Which of the following definitions are *correct* and *complete*?

1   A mole of a substance is the amount of that substance which contains a number of identical particles equal to the Avogadro constant.
2   The Avogadro constant is equal to the number of atoms in exactly 12 g of ^{12}C.
3   The molar mass of a substance is the mass which reacts directly or indirectly with exactly 12 g of ^{12}C.

E 3.9   The *PVT* diagram for a condensable gas is shown below.

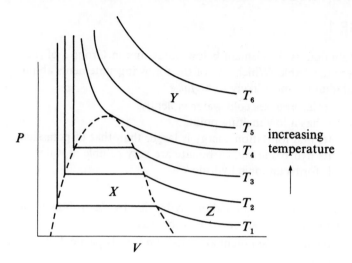

Which of the following statements are true?
1   In region X only liquid is present.
2   In region Y both gas and liquid co-exist.
3   In region Z only gas is present.

E 3.10   The lattice energy (enthalpy) of the ionic compound XY depends
upon
1   the ionic radii of the ions in XY.
2   the charges on the ions in XY.
3   the crystal structure of XY.

SECTION F INORGANIC AND ORGANIC CHEMISTRY

EXERCISE 1

F 1.1   Rubidium is the element below potassium in Group I of the
Periodic Table. Which one of the following statements about
rubidium is most likely to be *false*?

A   It decomposes cold water violently.
B   It has a low melting point.
C   Its first ionisation energy is larger than that of potassium.
D   Its hydroxide and carbonate are very soluble in water.
E   It forms an ionic hydride.

F 1.2   In the manufacture of sodium hydroxide by electrolysis of brine, a
flowing mercury cathode is used because

A   the discharge potential of sodium ions is particularly low on
mercury.
B   hydrogen ions have a large over-voltage on mercury.
C   chloride ions discharge in preference to hydroxide ions when a
mercury cathode is used.
D   sodium amalgam does not react with water.
E   chlorine gas does not react with mercury.

F 1.3   Compared with rhombic sulphur, monoclinic sulphur has a lower

A   melting point.
B   boiling point.
C   solubility in carbon disulphide.
D   reactivity.
E   stability at room temperature.

F 1.4   The corrosion (rusting) of iron in the presence of water can be most
effectively slowed down by

A   connecting the iron to magnesium.
B   connecting the iron to copper.
C   adding alkali until the pH of the water is 10.
D   adding acid until the pH of the water is 4.
E   adding an oxidising agent to the water.

F 1.5

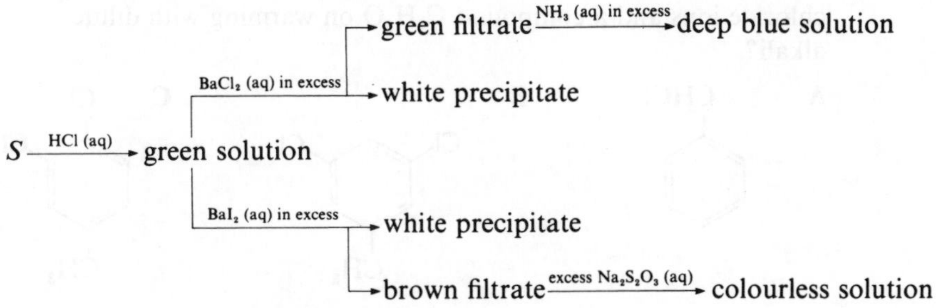

green filtrate $\xrightarrow{\text{NH}_3 \text{ (aq) in excess}}$ deep blue solution

$\xrightarrow{\text{BaCl}_2 \text{ (aq) in excess}}$ white precipitate

$S \xrightarrow{\text{HCl (aq)}}$ green solution

$\xrightarrow{\text{BaI}_2 \text{ (aq) in excess}}$ white precipitate

brown filtrate $\xrightarrow{\text{excess Na}_2\text{S}_2\text{O}_3 \text{ (aq)}}$ colourless solution

The salt S in the above scheme of reactions could be

A chromium(III) chloride.
B copper(II) chloride.
C copper(I) sulphite.
D copper(II) sulphate.
E chromium(III) sulphate.

F 1.6   The two-stage reaction sequence given below shows a possible
mechanism for the reaction between hydroxide ions and ethanoyl
(acetyl) chloride.

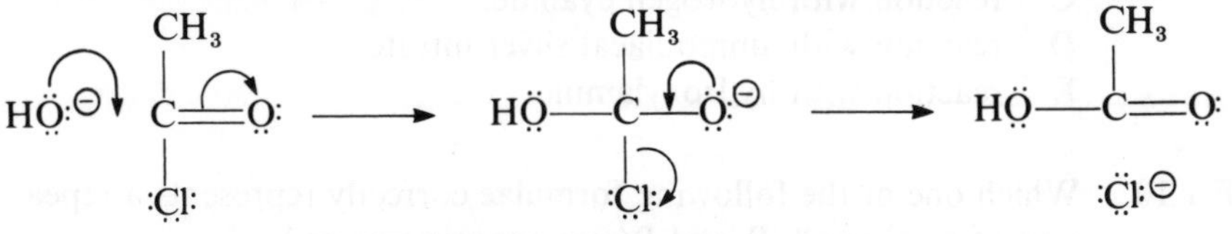

The *overall* reaction should be classified as

A electrophilic addition.
B nucleophilic addition.
C electrophilic substitution.
D nucleophilic substitution.
E elimination.

F 1.7   An alkene, C_6H_{12}, was treated with trioxygen (ozone) and then
water was added. The only product was propanone (acetone). The
structure of the alkene was

A $CH_3CH_2CH{=}CHCH_2CH_3$
B $(CH_3)_3CCH{=}CH_2$
C $(CH_3)_2C{=}C(CH_3)_2$
D $CH_3CH_2CH_2CH{=}CH_2$
E $CH_3CH_2CH{=}C(CH_3)_2$

F 1.8   Which one of the following compounds would be expected to give chloride ions and a compound C_7H_6O on warming with dilute alkali?

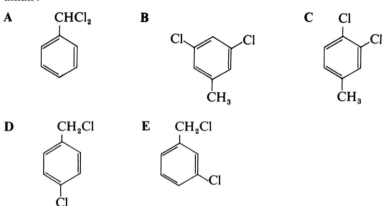

A   CHCl$_2$

B

C   Cl

D   CH$_2$Cl

E   CH$_2$Cl

F 1.9   Propanone (acetone) and ethanal (acetaldehyde) may be distinguished from one another by

A   the iodoform (tri-iodomethane) test.
B   reaction with 2,4-dinitrophenylhydrazine.
C   reaction with hydrogen cyanide.
D   reaction with ammoniacal silver nitrate.
E   reaction with hydroxylamine.

F 1.10   Which one of the following formulae correctly represents a repeat unit of a protein? (R and R′ are organic groups.)

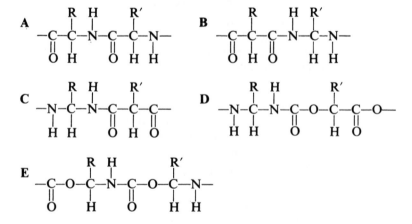

EXERCISE 2

F 2.1 A compound X evolves oxygen on heating. X dissolves in nitric acid and the solution gives a white precipitate with hydrochloric acid. This precipitate is soluble in sodium thiosulphate solution and in aqueous ammonia. X could be

    A Ag_2O B $Pb(NO_3)_2$ C HgO
    D Pb_3O_4 E $KClO_3$

F 2.2 How does copper metal react with nitric acid?

    A   It reacts with concentrated nitric acid to give mainly dinitrogen oxide (nitrous oxide).
    B   It reacts with moderately dilute nitric acid to give mainly dinitrogen oxide.
    C   It reacts with concentrated nitric acid to give mainly nitrogen monoxide (nitric oxide).
    D   It reacts with moderately dilute nitric acid to give mainly nitrogen monoxide.
    E   It reacts with very dilute nitric acid to give mainly nitrogen dixoide.

F 2.3 X is a pale coloured liquid at 0 °C. When warmed it gives off a vapour which grows progressively deeper in colour as the temperature is raised, but increasing the pressure at a given temperature has the opposite effect. When the vapour is passed into an aqueous solution of sodium hydroxide two different salts are formed simultaneously. What is X likely to be?

    A PCl_3 B PCl_5 C NO_2
    D N_2O_3 E N_2O_4

F 2.4   A substance X, containing a Group IV element, has the reactions
and properties shown in the following diagram.

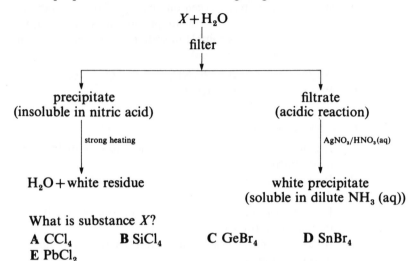

What is substance X?

A CCl_4 B $SiCl_4$ C $GeBr_4$ D $SnBr_4$
E $PbCl_2$

F 2.5   When the carbon–carbon double bonds in molecules of the
compound Q are broken by oxidation, the formulae of the main
organic products are CH_3CO_2H and $CH_3CH_2COCH_3$.
Which one of the following structures could be that of Q?

A

$$CH_3CH_2CH_2 \diagdown \diagup H$$
$$C=C$$
$$H \diagup \diagdown CH_3$$

B

$$CH_3 \diagdown \diagup H$$
$$C=C$$
$$CH_3 \diagup \diagdown CH_2CH_3$$

C

$$CH_3 \diagdown \diagup CH_2CH_2CH_3$$
$$C=C$$
$$H \diagup \diagdown CH_3$$

D

$$CH_3CH_2 \diagdown \diagup H$$
$$C=C$$
$$CH_3 \diagup \diagdown CH_3$$

E

$$CH_3 \diagdown \diagup H$$
$$C=C$$
$$H \diagup \diagdown CH_2CH_3$$

F 2.6   Propanonitrile, CH_3CH_2CN, may be made by the reaction of
cyanide ions with bromoethane (ethyl bromide). Which one of the
following statements is *not* correct?

A   The cyanide ion is acting as a nucleophile.
B   The reaction is an example of a good method for making
nitriles.
C   The reaction is a substitution reaction.
D   The reaction requires a catalyst.
E   Bromide ion is formed during the reaction.

F 2.7   The three-stage reaction sequence given below shows a possible
mechanism for the hydrolysis of methyl ethanoate (acetate).

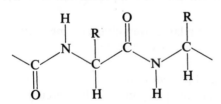

The overall reaction should be classified as

A   electrophilic addition.
B   nucleophilic addition.
C   electrophilic elimination.
D   electrophilic substitution.
E   nucleophilic substitution.

F 2.8   The structural unit

is found in molecules of

A   cellulose.   B   nylon.   C   proteins.
D   poly(esters).   E   amino acids.

F 2.9   The base strengths of ammonia and ethylamine are different because of the electron-releasing properties of the ethyl group. Which one of the following pairs correctly shows the effect of the ethyl group?

	effect on strength of $C_2H_5NH_2$ as a base relative to NH_3	effect on strength of $C_2H_5NH_3^+$ as an acid relative to NH_4^+
A	increase	increase
B	increase	decrease
C	decrease	decrease
D	decrease	increase
E	increase	no change

F 2.10   A compound which yielded ammonia with ice-cold sodium hydroxide solution could be

A   ethanamide (acetamide).
B   ammonium ethanoate (acetate).
C   aminoethanoic acid (glycine).
D   ethylamine.
E   urea.

EXERCISE 3

F 3.1   Hydrogen is *not* given off at a flowing mercury cathode during the electrolysis of brine in the commercial production of sodium hydroxide because

A   hydrogen ions have a large overvoltage on mercury.
B   sodium ions have a large overvoltage on mercury.
C   the hydrogen ions react with the water to form H_3O^+.
D   there is an iron grid present in the mercury to prevent this.
E   the hydrogen forms an amalgam with the mercury.

F 3.2   Which one of the following conversions involves an oxidation of vanadium (symbol V)?

A $VO^{2+} \rightarrow VO_2^+$
B $VF_5 \rightarrow V_2O_5$
C $VO_2^+ \rightarrow VO_4^{3-}$
D $VO^{2+} \rightarrow V^{3+}$
E $K_2VCl_6 \rightarrow V(NH_3)_6Br_3$

F 3.3 X is a dark brown powder which turns to a yellow solid on heating
and yields a gas which relights a glowing wood splint. When X is
heated with concentrated hydrochloric acid, a white solid is formed
and a gas is given off which bleaches moist litmus paper. The white
solid is soluble in hot water but only sparingly soluble in cold
water. Which one of the following compounds could be X?

A MnO_2 B $Pb(NO_3)_2$ C BaO_2
D PbO_2 E $CuO_2 . H_2O$

F 3.4   When an excess of chlorine gas reacts with hot, concentrated
aqueous sodium hydroxide solution, what chlorine-containing
sodium salts are formed?

A   chloride and chlorate(I) (hypochlorite)
B   chlorate(V) (chlorate) only
C   chloride only
D   chloride and chlorate(V)
E   chlorate(I) only

F 3.5   The reaction of bromine with ethene (ethylene) is an example of

A   free-radical addition.
B   electrophilic substitution.
C   electrophilic addition.
D   nucleophilic substitution.
E   nucleophilic addition.

F 3.6   When heated with an excess of dilute aqueous hydrochloric acid,

the diester $\begin{array}{c} CH_2OCOCH_3 \\ | \\ CH_2CO_2CH_3 \end{array}$ would give

A $\begin{array}{c} CH_2OH \\ | \\ CH_2OH \end{array}$ B $\begin{array}{c} CH_2OH \\ | \\ CH_2CO_2CH_3 \end{array}$ C $\begin{array}{c} CH_2OCOCH_3 \\ | \\ CH_2CO_2H \end{array}$

D $\begin{array}{c} CH_2OH \\ | \\ CH_2CO_2H \end{array}$ E $\begin{array}{c} CH_2CO_2H \\ | \\ CH_2CO_2H \end{array}$

F 3.7   Molybdenum lies directly below chromium in the Periodic Table, so
it would be expected to

1   be a lustrous metal with a high density and high melting point.
2   be made passive by concentrated nitric acid.
3   form an acidic oxide, MoO_3.

F 3.8   Ethene (ethylene) can be prepared in the laboratory from ethanol and

1   concentrated hydrochloric acid.

2   concentrated sulphuric acid.

3   concentrated phosphoric(v) acid.

F 3.9   The compound of formula $NH_2CH_2CO_2H$ can be obtained

1   as optically active isomers.

2   by the action of ammonia on ethanoic (acetic) acid.

3   from the hydrolysis of protein.

F 3.10   The reaction of a base with 2-bromopropane (isopropyl bromide) under suitable conditions can lead to the formation of

1   propane.

2   propene (propylene).

3   propan-2-ol (isopropyl alcohol).

SECTION G REVISION EXERCISES (ALL TOPICS)
EXERCISE 1

G 1.1 The lines of the simple emission spectrum of an element are caused by electrons

A jumping from an orbital of one atom to the orbital of another atom.

B colliding with the nucleus.

C colliding with one another in orbit.

D jumping from one orbital to another orbital at a lower energy level in the same atom.

E jumping from one orbital to another orbital at a higher energy level in the same atom.

G 1.2 Boron trifluoride has zero dipole moment while ammonia has a dipole moment of 1.5 D because

A there is no possibility of hydrogen bonding in BF_3.

B BF_3 is pyramidal in shape while NH_3 is planar.

C NH_3 is pyramidal in shape while BF_3 is planar.

D boron is more electropositive than nitrogen.

E fluorine is more electronegative than hydrogen.

G 1.3 Under what conditions does a real gas behave most nearly as an ideal gas?

A at low pressures and low temperatures

B at low pressures and high temperatures

C at high pressures and low temperatures

D at high pressures and high temperatures

E near their critical pressures and temperatures

G 1.4   Which one of the following graphs would be obtained, for a particular temperature, on plotting the proportion of gas molecules with a particular speed (y-axis) against the speed of the molecules (x-axis)?

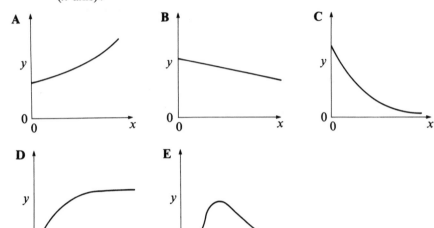

G 1.5   Tungsten is a catalyst for the decomposition of ammonia.

$$NH_3(g) \rightleftharpoons \tfrac{1}{2}N_2(g) + \tfrac{3}{2}H_2(g) \quad \Delta H^{\ominus} = +46 \text{ kJ mol}^{-1}$$

In the absence of a catalyst, the activation energy for this reaction is 335 kJ mol^{-1}.
Which one of the following statements about this reaction is *not* correct?

A   The activation energy for the decomposition in the presence of tungsten will be less than 335 kJ mol^{-1}.
B $\Delta H^{\ominus}$ for the synthesis of two moles of ammonia is -92 kJ.
C   Tungsten is a catalyst for the synthesis of ammonia.
D   The activation energy for the synthesis of ammonia, in the absence of a catalyst, will be 335 kJ mol^{-1}.
E   The standard enthalpy of formation of ammonia is -46 kJ mol^{-1}.

G 1.6   In which one of the following crystalline solids does the element exist as small molecules?

A   aluminium   B   carbon   C   lead
D   silicon   E   sulphur

G 1.7   An element P gave hydrogen gas when added to dilute hydrochloric
         acid at room temperature: it also gave the same gas when treated
         with aqueous sodium hydroxide at room temperature. Which one
         of the following could be P?

A   copper   B   lead   C   iron
D   phosphorus   E   aluminium

G 1.8   What happens when methane is mixed in the dark with three times
         its own volume of chlorine at room temperature?
A   There is no reaction.
B   Carbon and HCl are formed.
C CCl_4 and HCl are formed.
D $CHCl_3$ and HCl only are formed.
E CH_3Cl, CH_2Cl_2, $CHCl_3$ and HCl are formed.

G 1.9   An organic compound Y has a relative molecular mass of 60. It
         reacts with sodium hydroxide solution to give a soluble product.
         When treated with phosphorus pentachloride, it produces an
         organic compound that reacts vigorously with water.
         [Relative atomic masses: H, 1; C, 12; O, 16; F, 19.]
         What is the structural formula of Y?

A
$$H-\overset{\displaystyle H}{\underset{\displaystyle H}{C}}-C\overset{\displaystyle O}{\underset{\displaystyle O-H}{}}$$

B
$$H-\overset{\displaystyle H}{\underset{\displaystyle H}{C}}-\overset{\displaystyle H}{\underset{\displaystyle H}{C}}-\overset{\displaystyle H}{\underset{\displaystyle H}{C}}-O-H$$

C
$$\overset{\displaystyle H}{\underset{\displaystyle H}{}}C=\overset{\displaystyle H}{\underset{\displaystyle H}{C}}-\overset{\displaystyle H}{\underset{\displaystyle H}{C}}-F$$

D
$$H-\overset{\displaystyle H}{\underset{\displaystyle H}{C}}-\overset{\displaystyle H}{\underset{\displaystyle O}{C}}-\overset{\displaystyle H}{\underset{\displaystyle H}{C}}-H \quad \underset{\displaystyle H}{}$$

E
$$H-C\overset{\displaystyle O}{\underset{\displaystyle O-\overset{\displaystyle H}{\underset{\displaystyle H}{C}}-H}{}}$$

G 1.10 $RC\equiv N$, when heated with dilute sulphuric acid, gives
A $RCH{=}NH$ B RCO_2H C RSO_3H
D   ROH   E $ROSO_3H$

EXERCISE 2

G 2.1   The enthalpy change of formation of carbon dioxide gas is
-393 kJ mol^{-1} and that of water vapour is -286 kJ mol^{-1}. The
enthalpy change of combustion of one mole of ethanol is
-1369 kJ mol^{-1}. What is the enthalpy change of formation of one
mole of ethanol from its constituent elements?

A -690 kJ   B   118 kJ   C   690 kJ
D   275 kJ   E -275 kJ

G 2.2   The dissociation constant of ethanoic (acetic) acid is
1.80×10^{-5} mol dm^{-3} at 25 °C. What is the pH of a solution which
contains 1 mole each of ethanoic acid and sodium ethanoate in
10 dm^3?

A   4.75   B   5.26   C   5.75   D   6.26   E   6.75

G 2.3   Which one of the following compounds might yield the titration
curve shown below? (The curve represents complete neutralisation.)

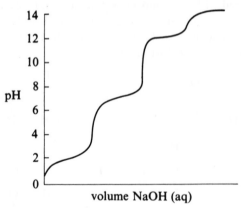

A H_3PO_3 B H_3PO_4 C $H_4P_2O_7$ D $H_2S_2O_3$
E H_5IO_6

G 2.4   Under like conditions, carbon monoxide competes 200 times more
effectively than oxygen for haemoglobin available in blood. The
effects in the body of carboxyhaemoglobin are detectable when it
reaches 5% of the concentration of oxyhaemoglobin in the blood.
Air contains 20% of oxygen by volume.
By using these data, it can be deduced that the minimum
concentration (parts per million, p.p.m.) of carbon monoxide in the
atmosphere that will result in detectable effects in the body is

A   10 p.p.m.   B   50 p.p.m.   C   250 p.p.m.
D   500 p.p.m.   E   1000 p.p.m.

G 2.5   The equilibrium constants K_p for the following reactions at a certain temperature T are

$$Fe(s) + CO_2(g) \rightleftharpoons FeO(s) + CO(g); \quad K_p = \tfrac{3}{2}$$
$$Fe(s) + H_2O(g) \rightleftharpoons FeO(s) + H_2(g); \quad K_p = \tfrac{5}{2}$$
$$CO(g) + H_2O(g) \rightleftharpoons CO_2(g) + H_2(g); \quad K_p = x$$

The value of x is

A   not calculable from the data given   B $\tfrac{4}{15}$
C $\tfrac{3}{5}$ D $\tfrac{5}{3}$ E $\tfrac{15}{4}$

G 2.6   When hydrogen sulphide is passed into an aqueous solution of cadmium(II) ions, Cd^{2+}, a yellow precipitate of cadmium(II) sulphide is obtained. This precipitate is also obtained in the presence of dilute hydrochloric acid but not in the presence of concentrated hydrochloric acid nor of an excess of potassium chloride.
Of the possible explanations given below, the only one which can account for all these observations is that

A   the presence of a high concentration of H^+ (aq) suppresses the ionisation of H_2S (aq).
B Cd^{2+} (aq) ions react with Cl^- (aq) to form covalent $CdCl_2$.
C   the concentration of S^{2-} (aq) is reduced by the formation of SCl_4^{2-} (aq).
D   CdS(s) is soluble in concentrated HCl (aq).
E Cd^{2+} (aq) ions react with Cl^- (aq) to form the complex ion $CdCl_4^{2-}$ (aq).

G 2.7   A solution of a sodium salt is warmed with dilute hydrochloric acid and a brown gas is evolved. This indicates the presence of

A   nitrite.   B   bromide.   C   chloride.
D   nitrate.   E   sulphite.

G 2.8   When an alcohol X is treated with hot acidified aqueous potassium manganate(VII) (permanganate), the final oxidation product gives the tri-iodomethane (iodoform) reaction. Which one of the following formulae could correspond to X?

A $C_6H_5CH_2OH$ B C_2H_5OH C $CH_3CH(OH)C_2H_5$

D $C_6H_5CH(OH)C_2H_5$ E   —OH

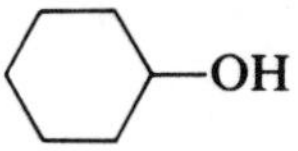

G 2.9 The repeat unit of *Terylene* can be represented by the following formula.

$$\left[OC - \hspace{-0.5em}\left\langle \hspace{-0.5em} \bigcirc \hspace{-0.5em} \right\rangle \hspace{-0.5em} - CO_2CH_2CH_2O \right]$$

The complete hydrolysis of *Terylene* with boiling aqueous sodium hydroxide results in the formation of

A $NaO_2C - \hspace{-0.3em}\left\langle \bigcirc \right\rangle \hspace{-0.3em} - CO_2Na$ and $HOCH_2CH_2OH$

B $NaOC - \hspace{-0.3em}\left\langle \bigcirc \right\rangle \hspace{-0.3em} - CONa$ and $HOCH_2CH_2OH$

C $NaO - \hspace{-0.3em}\left\langle \bigcirc \right\rangle \hspace{-0.3em} - ONa$, CO_2, and $HOCH_2CH_2OH$

D $NaO_2C - \hspace{-0.3em}\left\langle \bigcirc \right\rangle \hspace{-0.3em} - CO_2Na$ and $NaOCH_2CH_2ONa$

E $NaO_2C - \hspace{-0.3em}\left\langle \bigcirc \right\rangle \hspace{-0.3em} - CO_2CH_2CH_2OH$

G 2.10   Chlorine is passed into boiling methylbenzene (toluene) in the
          absence of a halogen carrier. The product X of this reaction gives
          on hydrolysis a compound Y, which gives a precipitate of copper(I)
          oxide with Fehling's solution. What are X and Y?

	X	Y
A	CH_3, Cl (ortho-substituted benzene)	CH_3, OH (ortho-substituted benzene)
B	CH_2Cl (benzene)	CH_2OH (benzene)
C	CH_2Cl (benzene)	CHO (benzene)
D	$CHCl_2$ (benzene)	CHO (benzene)
E	CCl_3 (benzene)	CO_2H (benzene)

EXERCISE 3

G 3.1   Why does ammonium nitrate lower the temperature of water in which it is being dissolved?

  A   It has a negative lattice energy (enthalpy).
  B   The lattice energy (enthalpy) is greater than the enthalpy of solvation of the ions.
  C   The strength of the bond between ammonium and nitrate ions in the crystal is greater than that between ammonium and hydroxide ions in solution.
  D   Six bonds have to be broken in the crystal and only one is formed in solution.
  E   The vapour pressure over a salt solution is always less than that of the pure solvent, so the temperature must fall.

G 3.2   An aliphatic compound gives (*a*) a salt, but no ammonia, with cold or hot aqueous alkali, (*b*) an ethanoyl (acetyl) derivative, (*c*) a copper(II) derivative when treated with aqueous copper(II) ethanoate (acetate), (*d*) a hydrochloride. The compound is therefore similar to

  A $C_6H_5NH_2$ B $CH_3CO_2NH_4$ C $H_2NCH_2CO_2H$
  D CH_3CONH_2 E $CH_3CH_2NH_2$

G 3.3   Two pure liquids X and Y have vapour pressures at 25 °C of 12.9 kPa and 26.8 kPa, respectively, and form an ideal mixture. What is the vapour pressure of a mixture containing two moles of X and one mole of Y at 25 °C?

  A   17.5 kPa   B   19.9 kPa   C   22.2 kPa
  D   39.7 kPa   E   52.6 kPa

G 3.4   The reaction of iodine with propanone (acetone) in aqueous solution is acid-catalysed, and the reaction is first order with respect to the hydrogen ion concentration. Keeping all other conditions the same, the ratio

$$\frac{\text{reaction rate at pH 1}}{\text{reaction rate at pH 2}}$$

will be

  A   10   B   2   C   1   D   0.5   E   0.1

G 3.5   Which one of the following reactions is characteristic of aluminium hydroxide?

A   It reacts with sulphuric acid to give a white precipitate of aluminium sulphate.

B   It fumes in the presence of hydrochloric acid because volatile aluminium chloride is formed.

C   It reacts with hydrochloric acid to give a white precipitate of aluminium chloride.

D   It reacts with aqueous sodium hydroxide to give a white precipitate of sodium aluminate.

E   It dissolves in aqueous sodium hydroxide to give a solution of sodium aluminate.

G 3.6   In separate experiments, 1 mol of the chlorides of the elements sodium to chlorine are each added to water. Which of the following diagrams best represents how the pH of the solutions so produced varies with the atomic numbers of the elements?

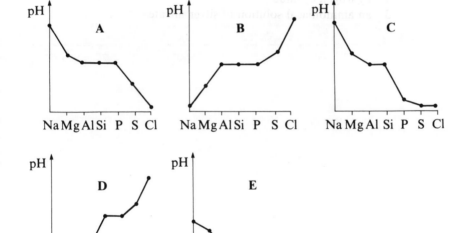

G 3.7 CH_3CN, when treated with lithium tetrahydridoaluminate ($LiAlH_4$), gives

A CH_3NH_2 B CH_3CONH_2 C $CH_3CH=NH$

D CH_3CH_2OH E $CH_3CH_2NH_2$

G 3.8 An example of an attack by an electrophilic reagent on an organic compound is the reaction between

    A methane and chlorine.

    B ethanoyl (acetyl) chloride and water.

    C bromoethane (ethyl bromide) and potassium cyanide.

    D ethene (ethylene) and bromine.

    E ethanal (acetaldehyde) and hydrogen cyanide.

G 3.9 Nitrogen monoxide, NO, and nitrogen dioxide, NO_2, are similar in that both

    1 are appreciably dimerised at room temperature.

    2 react at room temperature with aqueous sodium hydroxide.

    3 are reduced to nitrogen by hot copper.

G 3.10 With which of the following reagents do benzaldehyde and ethanal (acetaldehyde) react in a similar manner?

    1 aqueous sodium hydroxide

    2 hydrogen cyanide

    3 an ammoniacal solution of silver nitrate

Item Statistics and Correct Answers

For every multiple choice item in this book, the performance of the examination candidates has been analysed to provide a facility value and a discrimination index. These statistics, along with the correct options, are presented in the tables which follow.

The *facility value* of an item is the percentage of candidates who responded correctly (no mark is awarded to any candidate who chooses more than one option). The item's *discrimination index* is the (point-biserial) correlation[1] between success in responding to the item and score on the examination multiple choice test of which it was a part. Thus an item's discrimination index tends to be high when all those who do well on a test respond correctly to the item and when all those who do badly respond incorrectly or not at all. The maximum possible discrimination index is +1 and most of the items in the Advanced Level Chemistry examinations are intended to have discrimination indices greater than 0.25.

The average facility, and thus the average score of examination candidates on the items in this book, is approximately 57%. Of course, since A-level courses differ in content and emphasis, certain items will be less valid as tests of one course than of others, and teachers should bear this in mind, both in setting exercises for their students and in interpreting the results.

In the table on the following pages there will be found, under each item number, the letter for the correct option, the item's facility value and the item's discrimination index.

---

[1] The point-biserial correlation (r) is calculated as follows:

$$r = \frac{M_g - M_t}{\sigma_t} \left(\sqrt{\frac{p}{q}} \right)$$

where M_g = the mean total score on the test of the group choosing the correct option.
M_t = the mean total score on the test of the total sample.
p = the proportion of candidates choosing the correct option.
q = the proportion of candidates not choosing the correct option.
σ_t = the standard deviation of the total test score in the complete sample.

A1.1	A1.2	A1.3	A1.4	A1.5	A1.6	A1.7	A1.8	A1.9	A1.10
B	B	C	C	B	B	E	B	C	C
91%	85%	78%	76%	75%	74%	72%	69%	62%	60%
0.17	0.32	0.43	0.40	0.40	0.18	0.44	0.41	0.27	0.37

A2.1	A2.2	A2.3	A2.4	A2.5	A2.6	A2.7	A2.8	A2.9	A2.10
D	E	D	E	D	B	C	A	C	B
74%	71%	68%	65%	62%	59%	69%	64%	58%	50%
0.43	0.46	0.37	0.44	0.48	0.48	0.31	0.36	0.46	0.37

A3.1	A3.2	A3.3	A3.4	A3.5	A3.6	A3.7	A3.8	A3.9	A3.10
E	E	C	E	A	D	A	D	C	B
70%	62%	62%	55%	54%	52%	51%	51%	47%	35%
0.42	0.47	0.42	0.44	0.39	0.47	0.26	0.42	0.34	0.42

A4.1	A4.2	A4.3	A4.4	A4.5	A4.6	A4.7	A4.8	A4.9	A4.10
C	C	A	B	D	D	B	E	B	B
82%	53%	47%	47%	41%	41%	41%	33%	78%	71%
0.38	0.50	0.33	0.42	0.32	0.34	0.34	0.19	0.42	0.43

B1.1	B1.2	B1.3	B1.4	B1.5	B1.6	B1.7	B1.8	B1.9	B1.10
D	A	C	E	C	A	D	D	D	C
84%	79%	74%	72%	72%	72%	66%	64%	60%	58%
0.41	0.41	0.43	0.40	0.41	0.31	0.49	0.36	0.29	0.33

B2.1	B2.2	B2.3	B2.4	B2.5	B2.6	B2.7	B2.8	B2.9	B2.10
C	D	E	C	B	E	B	C	B	C
76%	71%	58%	56%	51%	36%	62%	56%	50%	44%
0.41	0.30	0.46	0.48	0.42	0.36	0.39	0.47	0.39	0.47

B3.1	B3.2	B3.3	B3.4	B3.5	B3.6	B3.7	B3.8	B3.9	B3.10
D	A	C	D	D	C	C	E	E	D
60%	59%	55%	52%	52%	51%	51%	39%	36%	33%
0.36	0.40	0.49	0.51	0.24	0.45	0.26	0.48	0.29	0.44

B4.1	B4.2	B4.3	B4.4	B4.5	B4.6	B4.7	B4.8	B4.9	B4.10
E	B	D	B	D	A	E	A	D	A
51%	48%	48%	47%	43%	32%	53%	31%	53%	42%
0.43	0.39	0.43	0.34	0.29	0.18	0.28	0.40	0.43	0.36

C1.1	C1.2	C1.3	C1.4	C1.5	C1.6	C1.7	C1.8	C1.9	C1.10
D	E	C	C	B	E	D	C	B	C
81%	76%	76%	73%	71%	69%	59%	59%	58%	52%
0.40	0.40	0.35	0.48	0.26	0.28	0.50	0.37	0.35	0.35

C2.1	C2.2	C2.3	C2.4	C2.5	C2.6	C2.7	C2.8	C2.9	C2.10
C	D	A	D	B	C	C	D	E	B
82%	74%	68%	67%	64%	62%	49%	46%	40%	34%
0.42	0.30	0.45	0.29	0.30	0.34	0.44	0.40	0.40	0.27

C3.1	C3.2	C3.3	C3.4	C3.5	C3.6	C3.7	C3.8	C3.9	C3.10
E	D	C	C	D	B	D	E	A	E
58%	54%	53%	49%	49%	49%	40%	40%	37%	30%
0.35	0.44	0.38	0.36	0.32	0.29	0.34	0.43	0.31	0.17

C4.1	C4.2	C4.3	C4.4	C4.5	C4.6	C4.7	C4.8	C4.9	C4.10
B	A	D	B	A	A	D	D	D	B
71%	58%	55%	42%	40%	38%	78%	77%	59%	54%
0.44	0.50	0.40	0.39	0.36	0.38	0.35	0.38	0.37	0.37

D1.1	D1.2	D1.3	D1.4	D1.5	D1.6	D1.7	D1.8	D1.9	D1.10
A	E	E	B	A	B	E	D	D	D
87%	82%	73%	72%	71%	66%	62%	62%	59%	38%
0.48	0.44	0.48	0.44	0.51	0.41	0.46	0.41	0.51	0.34

D2.1	D2.2	D2.3	D2.4	D2.5	D2.6	D2.7	D2.8	D2.9	D2.10
B	E	E	D	C	E	E	E	A	C
82%	75%	68%	65%	64%	63%	60%	59%	44%	40%
0.46	0.34	0.37	0.40	0.43	0.41	0.48	0.35	0.24	0.43

D3.1	D3.2	D3.3	D3.4	D3.5	D3.6	D3.7	D3.8	D3.9	D3.10
D	E	C	A	D	E	C	A	B	E
71%	61%	59%	51%	46%	42%	38%	38%	36%	22%
0.34	0.42	0.41	0.38	0.40	0.30	0.32	0.23	0.33	0.24

D4.1	D4.2	D4.3	D4.4	D4.5	D4.6	D4.7	D4.8	D4.9	D4.10
C	A	B	C	D	B	A	D	E	B
61%	52%	52%	50%	41%	32%	65%	59%	57%	40%
0.46	0.38	0.29	0.42	0.38	0.39	0.42	0.36	0.45	0.30

E1.1	E1.2	E1.3	E1.4	E1.5	E1.6	E1.7	E1.8	E1.9	E1.10
C	E	D	A	E	A	D	B	C	B
91%	81%	73%	73%	72%	71%	71%	69%	63%	63%
0.36	0.47	0.38	0.40	0.31	0.32	0.53	0.38	0.43	0.35

E2.1	E2.2	E2.3	E2.4	E2.5	E2.6	E2.7	E2.8	E2.9	E2.10
C	C	B	E	E	E	D	B	B	A
62%	62%	56%	53%	52%	48%	45%	42%	40%	37%
0.50	0.51	0.52	0.36	0.30	0.35	0.33	0.37	0.36	0.40

E3.1	E3.2	E3.3	E3.4	E3.5	E3.6	E3.7	E3.8	E3.9	E3.10
B	E	B	A	C	C	D	B	E	A
68%	61%	55%	51%	41%	36%	34%	75%	51%	36%
0.40	0.52	0.29	0.24	0.34	0.40	0.29	0.28	0.37	0.21

F1.1	F1.2	F1.3	F1.4	F1.5	F1.6	F1.7	F1.8	F1.9	F1.10
C	B	E	A	D	D	C	A	D	A
84%	78%	66%	62%	61%	85%	83%	78%	73%	51%
0.37	0.40	0.38	0.34	0.29	0.43	0.42	0.33	0.41	0.36

F2.1	F2.2	F2.3	F2.4	F2.5	F2.6	F2.7	F2.8	F2.9	F2.10
A	D	E	B	D	D	E	C	B	B
42%	42%	41%	39%	68%	66%	58%	50%	47%	41%
0.24	0.41	0.35	0.35	0.43	0.30	0.37	0.30	0.34	0.35

F3.1	F3.2	F3.3	F3.4	F3.5	F3.6	F3.7	F3.8	F3.9	F3.10
A	A	D	D	C	D	A	C	E	C
69%	53%	42%	42%	62%	56%	38%	58%	55%	50%
0.45	0.46	0.28	0.34	0.33	0.43	0.27	0.41	0.47	0.42

G1.1	G1.2	G1.3	G1.4	G1.5	G1.6	G1.7	G1.8	G1.9	G1.10
D	C	B	E	D	E	E	A	A	B
77%	67%	62%	55%	52%	69%	58%	60%	56%	44%
0.25	0.38	0.50	0.52	0.40	0.41	0.32	0.21	0.42	0.45

G2.1	G2.2	G2.3	G2.4	G2.5	G2.6	G2.7	G2.8	G2.9	G2.10
E	A	B	B	D	E	A	C	A	D
53%	44%	43%	41%	40%	43%	31%	49%	46%	45%
0.44	0.36	0.31	0.27	0.25	0.34	0.32	0.28	0.46	0.47

G3.1	G3.2	G3.3	G3.4	G3.5	G3.6	G3.7	G3.8	G3.9	G3.10
B	C	A	A	E	E	E	D	E	C
72%	56%	49%	29%	59%	15%	73%	69%	35%	44%
0.38	0.44	0.45	0.42	0.50	0.15	0.50	0.52	0.12	0.29

Simple completion items

(containing 5 options – **A, B, C, D** and **E**)

Choose *one* of the letters only to indicate the answer which you think is most suitable

Multiple completion items

(containing 3 statements – **1, 2, 3**)

Select the statements which you think are correct. Then answer according to the following code:

A   if you think **1, 2** and **3** are correct
B   if you think **1** and **2** only are correct
C   if you think **2** and **3** only are correct
D   if you think only **1** is correct
E   if you think only **3** is correct

(no other combination of statements is used for a correct answer)